Sheng Zhen

WUJI YUAN GONG
A Return to Oneness
Qigong of Unconditional Love

Rendered by Li Jun Feng

Disclaimer: The information presented in this book has been carefully researched and passed on to our best knowledge and conscience. Despite this fact neither the author nor the publisher assume any type of liability for presumed or actual damage to any person that might result from the direct application or use of the statements in this book. The information in this book is solely intended for interested readers and educational purposes.

Acknowledgements

The authors gratefully acknowledge the following persons:
Elena Cortez, Michelle Magsaysay, and Marie Phillips, for rewriting the instructions to the movements for this new and updated edition; Dr. Ma. Teresa M. Sicat, our copy editor for this edition, Anabel Alejandrino for reediting the book; and to all members of the International Sheng Zhen Society Foundation who lovingly gave of themselves in some form making it possible for this work of love to spread throughout the world.

聖 眞
無 極 元 功

國 際 聖 眞 協 會

Title of the original edition: SHENG ZHEN WUJI YUAN GONG *A Return to Oneness*
Copyright © 1996, 1998, 2002, 2003 International Sheng Zhen Society Foundation, Manila, Philippines
This work has been mediated by Schneelöwe Verlagsberatung & Verlag GmbH, Aitrang, Germany.

All rights reserved.
No part of this book may be reproduced in any form or by any means without a written permission from the copyright owner and publisher.
Photographs: by Tonio Garcia
Design by Ana Cristina de Borja-Araneta
Cover by Anabel V. Alejandrino

First English Edition 2004
© by Lotus Press
Box 325, Twin Lakes, WI 53181, USA
website: www.lotuspress.com
email: lotuspress@lotuspress.com
The Shangri-La Series is published in cooperation with Schneelöwe-Verlagsberatung, Federal Republic of Germany
© 2003 by Schneelöwe Verlagsberatung & Verlag, Aitrang, Germany

ISBN 0-914955-77-2
Library of Congress Control Number 2004102259
Printed in Germany

Sheng Zhen

WUJI YUAN GONG

A Return to Oneness

Qigong of Unconditional Love

Rendered by Li Jun Feng

INTERNATIONAL SHENG ZHEN SOCIETY FOUNDATION

LOTUS PRESS
SHANGRI-LA

Contents

- **From the Master** — VII
  Li Jun Feng

- **From the Editor** — XIII
  Anabel Alejandrino

- **Sheng Zhen** — XVIII

- **Zhongtian Movement** — 1

- **Basic Preparation Instructions** — 5

- **Zhongtian Yiqi** — 7
  Sitting Non-Moving Qigong

- **Jiu Zhuan Zhen Dan** — 11
  Nine Turns Non-Moving Lying Qigong
  Inspired by Lao Tzu

- **Kuan Yin Sitting Qigong** — 19
  1 Dragon Flying in the Clouds — 21
  2 Holy Dragon Returning to the Mountains — 23
  3 Cloudy Mountain Going Through the Mist — 25
  4 Qui Er Gazing At the Moon — 27
  5 The Union of Qi with Heaven — 29
  6 Holding the Lotus and Crossing the Ocean — 31
  7 Shadow from Buddha's Light — 33
  8 Parting the Clouds and Seeing the Sun — 35
  9 Boat Travelling in Buddha's Ocean — 37
  10 Looking to Heaven and Returning to Oneness — 39
  11 Returning to the Ninth Level of Heaven — 41
  12 Rain Shower of Apricot Blossoms — 43
  13 Opening and Closing of Bodhi — 45
  14 Qi Returns to One — 48
  15 Rising and Descending — 49
  16 Gathering Qi — 51

- **Kuan Yin Standing Qigong** — 53
  1 Boat Rowing in the Stream of Air — 55
  2 Travelling Eastward Across the Ocean — 57
  3 Praying to Heaven to Show the Way — 59
  4 Expelling Unhealthy Qi — 61
  5 Qui Er Gazing at the Moon — 63
  6 Qi Twirling Above the Head — 65
  7 Building Dan and Cultivating Xing — 67
  8 Overlooking the Ocean — 69
  9 Lotus Flower Going Through the Mountains — 71
  10 Qi Returns to the Dantian — 73
  The Closing Movement — 75

- **Jesus Sitting Qigong** — 77
  1 Love Descends on Me — 79
  2 Unraveling the Heart — 81
  3 Supreme Truth — 83
  The Closing Movement — 85

- **Jesus Standing Qigong** — 87
  1 Man Obtains Heaven and Its Powers — 89
  2 Returning to Heaven and Becoming One with Nature — 91
  3 Pouring Qi Into the Dantian — 93
  4 Bringing One to the Shore of Understanding — 95
  5 Contemplate and Reflect — 97
  6 Descending to Earth — 99
  7 Sheng Zhen Purifies the Person — 101
  8 The Bridge of Heaven's River — 103
  9 Looking Into the Depths of One's Heart — 105
  10 Looking at Life — 107
  11 Showing the Way to Better the Person — 109
  The Closing Movement — 111
  Conclusion — 112

- **Mohammed Sitting Qigong** — 117
  1. Beginnings and Endings Return to Heaven — 119
  2. Purifying the Center of the Heart — 121
  3. Entering the Heart — 123
  4. Attaining Pure Consciousness — 125
  5. Fulfillment — 127
  6. Moving Towards the Dantian — 129
  7. Freeing Oneself to Become a Saint — 131
  8. Walk to the Center of Heaven — 133
  9. Stirring the Clouds — 135
  10. The Heart is Clear Like Water — 137
     The Closing Movement — 139

- **Mohammed Standing Qigong** — 141
  1. Truth Unfolds Like a Flower — 143
  2. Body Leaps to the Lotus — 145
  3. Floating in a Mist to Truth — 147
  4. The Blending of Qi — 149
  5. Love Like the True Lord — 151
  6. Fly and Return in Peace — 153
  7. Man Embodies the Truth — 155
  8. Like Wind, Like Clouds — 157
  9. Pure Heart Descends — 159
  10. Perched on the Flying Crane — 161
      The Closing Movement: Love Comes from One — 163
      Conclusion — 164

- **Hui Chun Yidan (Return to Spring) Inspired by Lao Tzu** — 167
  1. The Spring Sun has Returned — 169
  2. Restoring the Sun to Its Origin — 171
  3. Rediscovering the Moon — 173
  4. Returning the Moon — 175
  5. The Source of Thought — 177
  6. Sunrise Brings Back the Light — 179
  7. Flying and Gazing at the Nine Levels of Heaven — 181
  8. Cultivate Your Dan and Higher Self — 183
  9. The Moon Rises and Shines on the West Chamber — 185
  10. The True Moonlight — 187
  11. The Reblooming of Spring Flower — 189
  12. Billowing Silk Like an Endless Road — 191
  13. The Universe Trembles — 193
  14. Qi Returns to Spring — 195
      The Closing Movement — 197

- **Glossary of Terms** — 198

About the Master — 200

From the Master

How It Began

My interest in the field of medicine and philosophy began early in my life. As a young man, I had a fascination for the dynamics of human relationships and the workings of the universe. Perhaps it was my grandfather, an accomplished Chinese doctor, who also influenced and inspired me. Because of my love for the natural sciences, after high school, I took an entrance exam to go to medical school. However, destiny has a way of arranging things. Although I was also interested in sports, I only saw it as a pastime. Yet, I ended up majoring in wushu (martial arts) in the Physical Education University. In time, I became the chief coach of the Beijing Wushu Team and the head coach of the People's Republic of China National Wushu Team. I enjoyed my life as a coach tremendously. During my career, my students garnered over 70 gold medals from national and international competitions. Our team was champion for twelve consecutive years in all of China.

In 1982, again because of circumstances and not by design, I was chosen to play the lead role in a much awaited movie even though I had no previous acting experience. It was then that my career as a movie actor took off with the film, "Wu Lin Zhi" (The Honor of Dong Fang Xu). The movie enjoyed tremendous success. I became an actor by day and a coach by night. Because of media exposure and other films I starred in, I became a household name. Fame and success followed me. All this brought excitement and joy to my life. But I always felt that there was still something missing. I knew what I yearned for was inner development and spiritual growth.

All throughout my coaching career, I learned qigong from many famous masters. At that time, although I did not really understand the essence of qigong, I knew that it was for inner cultivation. Continuously, I sought out one master after another, all of whom were more than willing to share their practice with a famous personality.

It was then that I met Master Gong Chang, a simple, little-known master from the countryside. Inner guidance told him to go to the city and find me to specifically tell me that I had a mission waiting to be fulfilled. In just thirty minutes, he taught me a simple form of meditation which I came to know later as **Zhongtian Yiqi Gong**. I practiced what he taught me and I knew even then that this was different from anything I had learned in the past. I was attracted not so much to the man as to the practice, the philosophy behind the practice, and how it made me feel.

Through daily practice, and its many facets, I could feel the oneness of Heaven, Earth, and Man. I experienced the entire universe within myself. Little by little, all my interests and focus in life slowly went towards this. Being told that I had a mission was strange to me but the fascination with this qigong continued to propel me forward. In time, through continuous practice, through divine inspiration while in meditation, the different forms and their accompanying contemplations and teachings unfolded.

Qigong of Unconditional Love

Often I am asked why the various forms are named after deities and leaders of different spiritual traditions? It is in our desire to honor them. The gifts of these spiritual entities — their philosophies, teachings, and what they represent are expressed in the movements and the contemplations that accompany the forms. They are the embodiment of Heaven, Earth, and Love.

Through the practice, I came to understand that love is the Source of All - love that is unconditional, selfless and totally free. It is from this that qi came into being, flowing out of unconditional love. From timelessness, from wuji, qi created the universe of non-definable reality. From this non-dual reality, yin and yang came into being and blended together giving rise to the world of duality. Wuji became taiji. So it is qi that created the universe and it is unconditional love that gave birth to qi.

In time, the different moving and non-moving forms came to be collectively known as **Sheng Zhen Wuji Yuan Gong** — Sheng Zhen, the highest most sacred truth, which is unconditional love. Sheng Zhen is kindheartedness. It is all good things in one — fraternal love, filial love, love for nature, love for oneself. All forms of love put together is Sheng Zhen. Sheng Zhen is the essence of the universe. It is the spirit that moves and permeates the practice of **Wuji Yuan Gong**. **Sheng Zhen Wuji Yuan Gong** is the original, most basic form of qigong. It is timeless. It is old but it is also new. It is old because the truth expressed in its philosophy always existed. It is new because it is expressed and imparted in a new way to suit the times.

In the beginning of man's existence on this realm, people were natural and simple. The material world had not yet developed, had not yet evolved. People were happy and naturally communed with nature. They spoke about love with ease because true love was everywhere. However, in today's modern technological society – although technology has been proficient in bringing about many material benefits and modern conveniences, people have become excessively busy and competitive. Everyone is constantly in a hurry leading to miscommunications and deep misunderstandings. People's lives are filled with worry, conflict and stress often creating an environment of callousness, ruthlessness, confusion and skepticism. These conditions have distanced people from the natural love that exists within their own hearts. This state of affairs has affected the human body's health leading to different ailments.

To have a healthy body, one must lead a happy life. The spirit and the emotions must be healthy. Practicing qigong, engaging in the exchange and interflow of qi with the universe, is as essential as eating is to the body. To have quality of life, one must practice any of the beneficial types of qigong offered in the world today. One such kind is **Sheng Zhen Wuji Yuan Gong**, practiced in its totality – both in form and in philosophy.

Sheng Zhen Wuji Yuan Gong has moving and non-moving forms. The moving forms help cultivate qi while the non-moving forms help condense and store the qi in the body. **Sheng Zhen Wuji Yuan Gong** has three main functions. First, it is good for physical health. The inner cultivation of qi helps improve the circulation of the blood and strengthens the body which directly improves your health. So it is medical qigong. Secondly, it is good for the emotions. It can remove stress, worries, nervousness, anger and hatred so that, no matter what is going on around you, you are calm, at ease and balanced. Therefore, it is emotional qigong. Thirdly, **Sheng Zhen Wuji Yuan Gong** opens and purifies the heart and elevates the spirit so it is spiritual qigong.

In a short period of time, as I grew into the practice, it became the focus of my life. I came to understand and feel the uniqueness of this particular form of qigong and its power to transform lives. Through the practice, **I have experienced how love can make everything happen. Love can transform people's hearts. Love can dissolve hate. Love can affect the environment. Unconditional love is the best medicine and the highest power. I have learned that the true purpose of man's life is to learn to love and give love. It is this purpose that Sheng Zhen Wuji Yuan Gong serves because in this qigong, love and qi are never separate.**

Because of the countless blessings I have received through this practice, I want others to benefit from it as well. I want to devote my life to sharing this invaluable gift so that others too may be blessed. Whenever I return to China, my colleagues tell me how foolish I am for giving up the prestige and the recognition I had as an actor and head coach only to teach qigong. I tell them that to me there is nothing more important than qigong – no money, no fame, because qigong can help people. Qigong can help uplift society.

Sharing the Practice

In order to promote the spirit of Sheng Zhen and share the practice of **Sheng Zhen Wuji Yuan Gong** with the world, the International Sheng Zhen Society was formed in 1995. Shortly thereafter, in 1996, I started to travel around the world. In devoting all my time in helping others experience its benefits, I have seen how people truly love this form of qigong.

From their own personal experiences, they have seen that it is a medical, emotional and spiritual qigong. Not only has the practice helped their bodies but it has also changed how they view the world. Others have told me that without **Wuji Yuan Gong** they would not be able to endure the tremendous pressures of work and would have perhaps suffered a nervous breakdown if it had not been for the practice and the profound understanding of life that it brings. I also have heard of setbacks and challenges. Those who have been confronted with difficulties have been able to ride the tide and dissolve the conflict, hatred and anxiety because of their experience of Sheng Zhen and the benefits they gained from doing the practices.

With practice, the wisdom of heart is revealed to you so that you are able to see the big picture, the long term. Temporary loss or gain does not make you lose your equanimity. You are able to remain self-possessed. You take all things calmly. This is what a natural life is. This is a life of perfect well-being.

In the Chinese tradition, filial piety is the most important value. Because of my work, I have had to leave the responsibility of looking after my aging mother to my wife. There have been times when I have been away from the family during difficult situations. Time and time again, believing in the power of love, I have seen our family emerge from a crisis confident in the wisdom of how life unfolds, feeling blessed, protected and supremely loved. Through the work, I have seen that when one surrenders to the spirit of Sheng Zhen, surrendering to the work of spreading love, everything comes into balance, everything moves in harmony.

How to Practice

The best way to learn **Wuji Yuan Gong** is doing it step by step, slowing immersing yourself in the practice. Learn the movements first. What is most important is that you allow your body to relax and that the different parts of your body move in harmony and are synchronized.

Whether the movements are big or small, fast or slow is immaterial. Simply follow your feeling. Be natural. Movements become natural and automatic with regular practice. In time, as you do the movements, as you relax the body more and more, you will begin to feel your qi flow. In Traditional Chinese Medicine, it is qi that leads the blood, that rules the blood. Now what is it that rules the qi? It is the power of an open heart.

Do not practice the movements only as exercise. The contemplations that accompany the movements complete the practice. Understanding the contemplations and practicing with feeling help deepen your experience of the movements and vice versa. It is this that opens the heart, that provides the key to open the door into a life of perfect well-being.

In the beginning of the practice, the mind leads the qi. Afterwards, as you practice regularly, you begin to notice that it is the qi that leads the mind. It is then that the practitioner learns to **listen** to the qi, to follow the qi, to follow the natural way of the heart. So when you listen to the qi and allow it to flow, your life too begins to flow with ease and you return to the natural state of wholeness.

Through the practice of **Sheng Zhen Wuji Yuan Gong**, learn to relax your body, relax your mind. For if a person does not know how to be at ease, they are, in a sense, suffering and cannot find the key. To rise above the shackles of this world, you must have the key. The key is your open heart. Only when the heart is open can the qi flow and make you truly happy and free.

Remember that the practice is like a small stream that slowly works its way to the ocean — always warm and gentle to the heart of the practitioner. Practice this qigong with the long term in mind. Do not be infatuated with quick, short-term results nor should you practice with expectations.

Sheng Zhen Wuji Yuan Gong is a philosophy for life. Through regular practice, one goes through the ups and downs of life seeing them as natural as the waves of the ocean, making life colorful and infinitely fascinating. When you practice **Wuji Yuan Gong** regularly, you experience a sense of equanimity and confidence that no matter what happens in life, you remain balanced and peaceful within.

Sheng Zhen Wuji Yuan Gong is movement and non-movement combined, internal as well as external, physical as a well as spiritual. It benefits the body and your life. The heart and the spirit return to simplicity and freshness. You can be in the present to enjoy every moment in life — to taste the fullness of life, its meaning, and profundity. Smiling sweetly to the world, may you spend every day of your life immersed in true joy and ease.

Li Jun Feng

From the Editor

I was first drawn to the Sheng Zhen practices because of the beauty of the movements and the desire to move like the master. The quality common to all the people I have always wanted to emulate is their ability to move with a certain ease and grace – the same ability found in a good athlete, dancer, or even one who can carve a turkey masterfully. For this very reason, I was attracted to Master Li Jun Feng, as his Taiji Quan student. When he first showed me the **Wuji Yuan Gong** movements, I can still remember how I initially thought that they looked easy to do because he made it look so effortless. I had no idea that to arrive at a perfect state of ease in the movements could take an entire lifetime.

As with anything beautiful and moving that you come across in life, it is a natural instinct to want to know more about it. It could be a person, a place, a way of life, or even a deeply moving work of art. When it is something infinitely fascinating, it inevitably has the power to transform the beholder – you study it, you watch it, you experience it. Its infinite facets continually challenge, expand, and, in the process, reveal more and more of you. The practice of **Sheng Zhen Wuji Yuan Gong** is one such thing. It is the spirit of Sheng Zhen – the spirit of unconditional love that empowers and makes the practice of **Wuji Yuan Gong** so fascinating and life-transforming. It is through the practice that one is led naturally into one's own perfect love in the heart. More than just being a healing tool for the body and the emotions, I have found that not only do the movements almost magically become the tools with which we can become the person we all want to be but also our capacity to enjoy life with its ups and downs is enhanced and magnified. Li Jun Feng is a living example of this.

The ease with which Master Li moves is the same ease with which he lives and faces challenges in life. He is so at ease with himself that one can sit next to him and feel perfectly comfortable not speaking. If I feel stressed and contracted on a particular day, all that evaporates at the sight of him running down the corridor from the kitchen to his room with his cheerful "Hi, Ana!". In that very moment, whatever responsibilities I am carrying become weightless. Immediately, I expand and am drawn into his space of no boundaries. That is the power of an open heart. It is infectious. It draws out what you intrinsically have within but sometimes forget.

Because of his mission to share the practices with the world, none of us who practice and teach are with Master Li for any length of time. He is never anywhere long enough for anyone to become too attached to him. But what we have at our beck and call is the practice itself. Although Master Li is the principal teacher for those of us who are fortunate enough to know him, the ultimate teacher is the practice itself. The guru is the qi in the form of the practice, so to speak. Our body is the medium of learning and the vessel of the unfolding gift as well. Our sincere efforts draw the divine grace, and our commitment and devotion to practicing provide the fuel for learning. As Teacher Li often reminds us, we come to know that the highest master is unconditional love.

It is an infinitely compassionate form of qigong. If what you want is a tool to maintain your health, that's what you get. If it is in your interest to be able to have enough energy to do your work well as a lawyer, a psychiatrist, a professor, a plant manager, or as head of state, that is what the practices will give you. If what you need is inspiration as an artist or writer, that's what you will receive. If being a good spouse is important to you, this too can be one of the benefits of doing the practices. If what you want is to overcome your fear of death and to ultimately merge with God and the universe, that's what you will be granted.

But there is another aspect to this qigong. Very often, even when an individual seems to have less than pure intentions when first embarking on the practices, so long as one practices with regularity, a little window in the heart is opened. And slowly, in a most natural way, the practitioner is transformed so that he or she is given even more than what he may have wished for at the start. In time, the heart begins to open up to the most profound gifts that the practices offer.

In the years that I have been teaching **Wuji Yuan Gong**, I have seen inhibited students who are primarily interested in good health become more free and at ease with themselves. I have seen shy and insecure personalities transform into shining examples of kindness and quiet confidence. I have seen one cured of an addiction without consciously wanting to be free of it. I have been at the deathbed of a once fearful person, beautifully immersed in the spirit of Sheng Zhen, the spirit of unconditional love, as he surrendered to his destiny with total faith and trust. Master Li himself, I have been told by former students from his coaching days, is a completely different person today. From someone who was demanding and exacting, whom everyone feared, he has become the lovable, understanding, and infinitely wise person we have come to know. Even his facial features have changed to reflect the inner transformation. When you have surrendered yourself totally to love, to the spirit of Sheng Zhen, there is no limit to how much one can attain.

In my teaching, it is very clear to me that it is the student's devotion to the practices that eventually brings about the benefits and the learning. Although the teacher provides the basic knowledge, she herself is in process which makes it possible for her to see first-hand the power of the practices. Seeing how she herself is changed by the practices, she can truly understand a student's growth and development. Like anything in life, it is what you have experienced that you can effectively share. And as in any form of education, you also learn from watching your students and listening to their insights. No two people are alike so the range of possibilities is limitless in a classroom setting. It is a divine exchange between student and teacher where both are transformed by the resulting energy in the exchange. The process in itself is qigong; the requirements to being a good teacher are the same as that of a student — commitment, belief in the process, belief in the qi, and belief in oneself.

It is the same when people practice as a group. There is an exchange of qi that takes place and something new is created in the process. It is not merely a case of adding two and two to get four. When even just four people practice together, the experience of the qi is magnified geometrically — an energy is created in the exchange.

The beautiful contemplations that accompany the movements are in themselves powerful in unlocking avenues of deeper understanding. Doing the movements enables one to understand the contemplations better; studying the contemplations give more meaning to the movements. The process removes inner barriers that exist between the heart, mind, and emotions and how these manifest themselves in the body. The practice also dissolves barriers we may have between ourselves and others. As a result, there is a growing appreciation for the body; we become more acquainted and familiar with it and how it relates to the mind and heart. One need not study the teachings to receive the benefits of the practice. But studying them enriches one's experience of the practice and deepens one's appreciation and understanding of what makes this form of qigong special.

When the first edition of this book was published, there was literally a handful of regular practitioners and Master Li was the only teacher. Today there are practitioners and teachers in all the continents and an ever-growing number of individuals who are reaping the harvest of this beautiful and moving practice. We, who have worked on this current edition with the master, are so blessed to have been given the honor of placing ourselves at the feet of the universe and opening our minds, hearts, and bodies to be able to update this book so that it can reach more people. Our years of practice and teaching have laid the foundation, giving us the confidence to know what we can share and see where we can still grow.

In conclusion, as one learns to let go so that the wisdom of the qi takes over, life's journey becomes a road of letting go of fears we hold in our bodies, concepts that render our minds inflexible, feelings in our hearts that we are attached to, and programming in our subconscious that hold us back. In so doing, we make way for what we truly are in essence – infinitely free beings, embodiments of love on every level, sparks of the divine, perfect and full. It is this experience that the practice of **Sheng Zhen Wuji Yuan Gong** brings. Ultimately, the practice is a key into one's own heart, which enables us to walk into one's own light. In the process, love for oneself becomes a tangible reality. This in turn leads to loving others unconditionally. These are the building blocks to a world of love – to a Sheng Zhen world.

Anabel Alejandrino

SHENG ZHEN

Within the depths of the human heart lies a paradise waiting to be experienced. It is the experience of Sheng Zhen – the experience of unconditional love. Sheng Zhen is pure, taintless, and totally free, depending on nothing for its existence. It is what every human being yearns for in his search for pleasure, happiness, peace, and contentment. It is man's ultimate quest. The human being can truly rest only when he has experienced the fullness of unconditional love in his heart. Often hoping to find answers to life's questions, he looks everywhere outside of himself to satisfy his needs. It is ironic that the very thing he is searching for is found resting in his heart.

Sheng Zhen is found in the heart of every human being as a seed waiting to be watered and nourished. Once Sheng Zhen is experienced in the heart, it is seen everywhere. There is nowhere that it does not exist, for the very fabric of existence is Sheng Zhen.

A glimpse of Sheng Zhen can shed light on the mystery of man's existence and his relationship with his fellowmen and the universe. A natural understanding of life and the order of the universe develops. Coming in touch with Sheng

Zhen affects and colors the way one sees and tastes life. In that love, the destructive power of differences and seeming inequalities is conquered; one's view of the world expands to embrace all. This is the power of unconditional love. It dissolves all conflicts and makes the light of truth shine; all differences melt in its luminosity and clarity. Sheng Zhen is the highest most sacred truth.

The experience of Sheng Zhen is the gift of the practice of Wuji Yuan Gong. Through the practice, the heart is opened; the experience of unconditional love becomes tangible and accessible. As the qi flows through the body in the practice, it brings about an experience of inner delight. This can only be described as being in a state of love. With time, one can even feel this blissful inner sensation while going through an ordinary day in one's life. Slowly and naturally, balance, harmony, wisdom, compassion, joy, and divine inspiration characterize one's existence.

To an individual whose being is permeated with Sheng Zhen, there is no such thing as a spiritual or materialistic life. There is only life and the beautiful poetry of existence in this realm. Such is the gift of Sheng Zhen.

中天動作

ZHONGTIAN MOVEMENT

The Zhongtian Movement symbolizes cleansing not only of the hands, the face, the body, but also of the spirit. Every Wuji Yuan Gong practice begins and ends with the Zhongtian Movement. At the beginning, it is a prayer for help and guidance in performing the practice; at the end, it is a prayer of gratitude for the help and guidance received.

When several different forms of Wuji Yuan Gong are practiced consecutively, it is not necessary to do the movement at the beginning and end of each form. Do it only at the beginning of the first form and at the end of the last form.

fig. 1　　　　　　　　　fig. 2　　　　　　　　　fig. 3

Instructions:

1. Raise both hands; bring them together with palms facing each other. Hands are slightly cupped with thumbs apart while tips of fingers and edge of hands touch (**Fig. 1**). Gently blow into the space between the palms.

2. Separate hands; simultaneously move right hand down to a slightly below the navel while moving left hand up to sweep the front of face from chin to forehead (**Fig. 2**).

3. Keeping right hand just below the navel, continue to move left hand, sweeping it downward in front of face and torso until it comes to rest on palm of right hand.

Elbows are slightly bent while upper arms are held slightly away from torso. Palms of hands are facing up and tips of thumbs are touching, forming a heart-shaped hollow space (**Fig. 3**).

fig. 1   fig. 2

Basic Preparation Instructions

Sitting Position Instructions:

The sitting forms of Wuji Yuan Gong are best done in full or half-lotus position (**Fig. 1**). If this position is too difficult, it is fine to simply sit in the easy pose with left ankle crossed on top of the right ankle. For those unable to assume any of these cross-legged positions, it is alright to sit on a chair provided that it allows one to sit upright and to firmly place both feet flat on the ground.

Keeping the torso straight and relaxed, hold head up, as if suspended from above.

Rest the hands, palms down on the knees.

It is important to be seated comfortably. If necessary, a cushion may be used when sitting on the floor. For some, a thin cushion tilting the pelvis slightly forward and higher than the knees may help in keeping the posture upright but relaxed.

Standing Position Instructions

Stand with feet about shoulder-width apart. Feet are parallel to each other. Do not lock knees. Elbows are slightly bent while upper arms are held slightly away from torso. Palms of hands are facing up and tips of thumbs are touching, forming a heart-shaped hollow space (**Fig. 2**).

Preparation:

Keeping head upright, slightly tuck in chin. The top of the head is aligned with the spine. Touch tip of tongue to upper palate; keep tongue in this position throughout the practice. Gently close eyes. Smile.

As the body relaxes, the breathing becomes even and light. You may come to feel as if you are hardly breathing. Feel as if you are breathing through your skin pores. Feel your body expanding, becoming larger and lighter until it is like smoke dissolving into the universe. Lose all sense of self. Remember to keep the body upright but relaxed. Pause in this state for some time; let your body become more and more relaxed before proceeding with this practice. Let the mind become still . . . become empty.

fig. 1

中天一氣

ZHONGTIAN YIQI

(Sitting Meditation)

Zhongtian Yiqi is a non-moving qigong that trains the mind. As this practice quiets the mind, one is able to return to the Beginning – to connect with Heaven, Earth, and with all humanity. Simply breathe lightly and naturally. This helps the body relax. Lose all sense of yourself. Forget everything. Free the mind of all worries and thoughts. With a tranquil and peaceful mind, one can go back to the beginning of time and see the world with renewed understanding.

Baihui 百會
Ni-Wuan 泥丸
Yin-Tang 印堂
Dantian 丹田

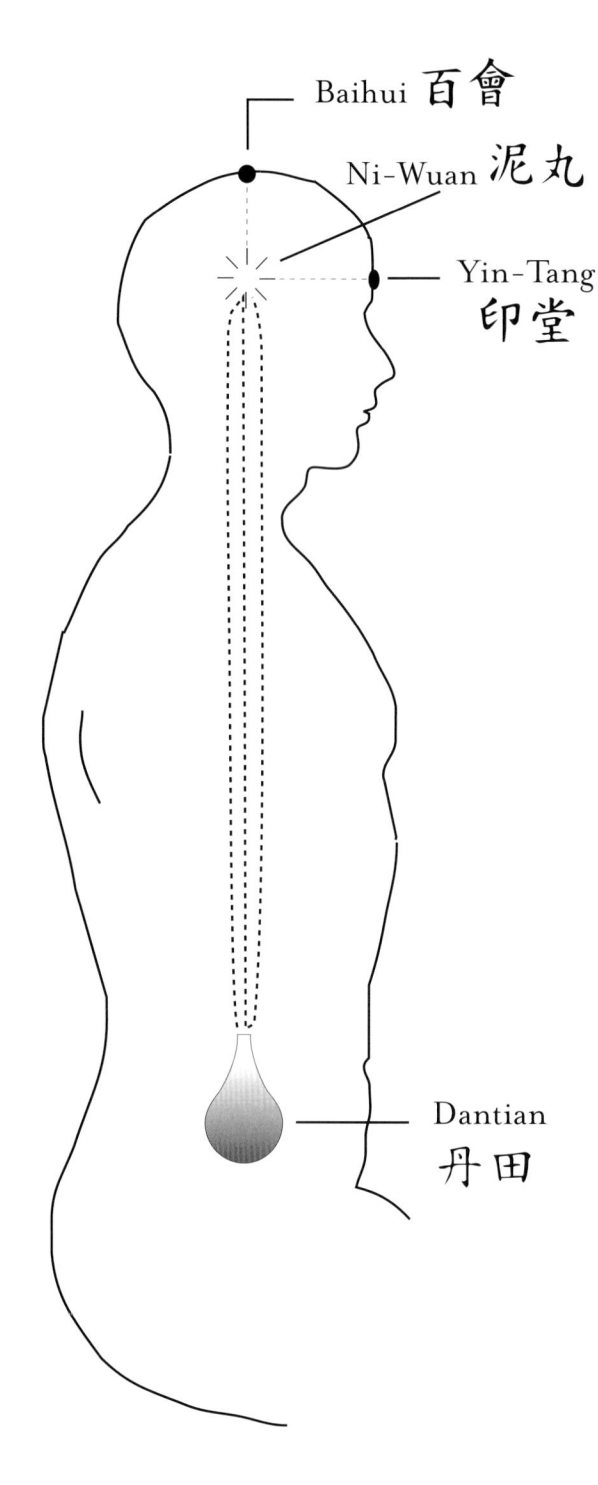

The Position:

Zhongtian Yiqi is best done in full or half lotus position (**Fig.1**). If this position is too difficult, it is fine to simply sit in the easy pose with left ankle crossed on top of the right ankle. For those who prefer to sit on a chair, what is important is that it allows one to sit upright and to firmly place both feet flat on the ground with knees about hip distance apart.

Keeping the torso straight and relaxed, hold head up, as if suspended from above.

Rest the hands, with palms down on the knees.

It is important to be seated comfortably. If necessary, a cushion may be used when sitting on the floor. For some, a thin cushion tilting the pelvis slightly forward and higher than the knees may help in keeping the posture upright but relaxed.

Preparation:

After establishing a proper posture, perform the **ZHONGTIAN MOVEMENT (see p. 3)**.

Zhongtian Yiqi Instructions:

1. Keeping the head upright, slightly tuck in the chin. The top of the head is aligned with the spine; the shoulders are wide. Touch tip of tongue to upper palate and keep tongue in that position throughout the practice. Gently close eyes and smile from within. Become aware of the *dantian;* keep your attention there for a while.

2. When you feel sufficiently relaxed, begin to visualize the qi moving from the *dantian* (point just below the navel) to the *ni-wuan* (point in the center of the head).

The *ni-wuan* is referred to as the gate of heaven and the *dantian* is likened to the bottom of the ocean. When the *qi* reaches the *ni-wuan*, pause briefly and offer a mental act of worship to whatever is your concept of the highest. Then move the qi back down to the *dantian*. Continue to visualize the qi gliding up and down – like smooth silk between the *dantian* and the *ni-wuan*.

3. Allow the qi to move up as you inhale and down as you exhale but do not use the breath to move the qi. The breathing should remain very light and very slow. This is possible when the body is very relaxed.

4. After some time, begin to keep the qi in the *ni-wuan* for longer periods before moving it back down to the *dantian*. Finally, let the qi remain in the *ni-wuan*. Once the qi has been connected to heaven, so to speak, it moves on its own very naturally. This is when you have dissolved into the universe (becoming the "void") and moved into a higher level of consciousness.

5. Now, focus only on the *ni-wuan*. It is here that the entire universe exists. Feel your entire being dissolve into the universe as you lose your feelings of individuality. You will naturally move into an even higher realm. Honor whatever you may see or feel at this point. Maintain a state of equanimity. Feel that you are immersed in a warm, nurturing, and loving environment.

Conclusion:

From the state of "voidness", gradually bring your awareness back to your body and slowly open your eyes, returning to your normal waking consciousness.

Allow the qi to return to the *dantian*. Conclude with the **ZHONGTIAN MOVEMENT (see p. 3)**.

Points to Remember:

1. Give yourself time before proceeding to do this practice. Allot sufficient time to establish a proper sitting posture and to become relaxed. Proceed slowly.

2. This is a non-moving form of **Wuji Yuan Gong**. The purpose of this qigong is to quiet the mind and to elevate the spirit.

3. While doing this qigong, let your heart be calm and your emotions happy. As you move the qi up and down feel that it is your love that is moving it. Feel your love spreading throughout the whole universe.

4. **Zhongtian Yiqi** can be done at any time. However, it is better done later in the evening when the qi is quiet.

5. This practice can be done alone but the benefits are greater when done with a group.

6. Gradually increase the length of your practice periods to increase your ability to sit for longer periods of time.

Contemplation

The significance of the position of the hands — Left hand is yang, right hand is yin. Yin is down, yang is up. This is the world. The thumbs touch to signify the harmony of things. The formation of the hands represents the shape of the heart. The space formed by the hands represents the empty world. You carry the empty world in your hands. Man's life is like the void that you see.

No matter how beautiful or repulsive the world appears to be, you must strive to find its essence. The only thing that man can really acquire in this life is an inner awakening. When man opens his heart and strives towards enlightenment, he finds the true meaning of life. The purpose of his existence unfolds.

This material world is not an end in itself; its true meaning can be found in this colorful world. Every bit of happiness and worry one experiences reveals an aspect of life. When you really come to an understanding of this world, you see that it is just an illusion — that it is empty inside. The only thing that one can leave behind in life is love for the world. The only thing that one can bring away is love in one's heart. The love you leave behind is the love you bring with you. They are one and the same.

Sitting here is so natural — as natural as the world outside your body. Only when you are empty can you experience tranquility and a loving heart. This is a naturally blissful state.

This empty world you hold in your hands corresponds to the true world in your niwuan. This is the essence and the only true point of existence of the empty world. Neither can be seen or grasped until your third eye is opened and until that world exists in your heart.

Although this qigong is simple, its meaning is very profound. In essence, "zhongtian" means to flow through freely — to be able to pass through without obstacles within yourself and others — to arrive at Oneness.

Reaching up to the heavens, reaching down to the earth, communicating with all of humanity — heaven, earth, and humanity are united as one. All are in constant movement.

九轉眞丹功
JIU ZUAN ZHEN DAN

(Nine Turns Lying Qigong)
Inspired by Lao Tzu

This meditative non-moving qigong involves the circulation of qi throughout the body to strengthen both the body and mind. Because this requires no physical effort, this can be practiced by those who are physically impaired.

The significance of the tongue's circling inside the mouth

Your tongue is the body of the heart
If the tongue moves, the mind follows
Qi moves in a circle along with the
    movement of the tongue
Directing movement of blood and qi
Balancing the jinglou and the blood

The movement of the tongue is akin
    to the movement of the heart
If the heart moves, the mind moves
If the mind moves, you become fire
    fire born from the mind
This fire enflames the whole body,
    all impurities are removed
Everything becomes light and pure.

Yang goes up
Allow the qi in the meridians and blood
    to circulate and balance
Pour qi into your body, your qi is your body
Mind controls the mind
Your spirit is your body.

The significance of qi circling around the navel

The navel is the boundary
Down is yang, up is yin
Yin and yang unite
The body naturally assimilates
    the circulating nutrients

The significance of the qi circulating around the body

The universe is in a state of constant
    transformation
always changing, never ending
No time, no limits
Your body is a place
In this place you can experience being
    a buddha
Empty…Empty…Nothing.

This never ends
So qi moves freely
Qi and blood can circulate with ease
This is how the universe, the stars, move

In the beginning, everything is hazy
Then heaven arises and earth descends
There is yin and yang
The work of harmony begins.

This is a high truth
No need to analyze
Beginning is hazy
Then eight (all) directions come to be.

Bring your heart and mind to a point
    of stillness
Do everything with sincerity
Quiet your heart, cultivate yourself
Become a buddha.

With a heart and mind that is focused
Everything becomes true
With a willful, worried, and restless heart
All can be lost -- everything becomes dust.

Everything is clear, clear is hazy
Buddha's way is difficult to understand
Everything is natural
Everything is true essence.

Preparation:

Lie flat on your back on a firm surface or cushion. Clothing should be loose and non-restrictive. Lay arms naturally at the sides, palms facing up, and gently close your eyes. Allow the mind to quiet down. Let go of worries. Let all thoughts subside.

Relax the body. Bring your awareness to the tense areas of the body and consciously relax those parts (such as the area between the eyebrows, area around the eyes, the neck and shoulders, arms, the small of the back, legs, etc.). The entire body should be very relaxed. Breathing is natural.

Refer to illustrations as you proceed.

Instructions:

1. With the mouth gently closed, lightly touch the inside of the mouth with the tip of the tongue as you move the tongue in circles. Begin by moving the tongue from the floor of the mouth up the left side, to the roof
of the mouth, then down the right side, and back to the floor of the mouth. Do this nine times.

As the tongue turns, simultaneously imagine and guide the qi starting from the *dantian* (area two inches below the navel) to make circles approximately the size of a saucer, around the navel: from left of navel, to above, and then to the right, then back to below navel. Circle also nine times. When the tongue is on the floor of the mouth, the qi should be at the *dantian* (below the navel). When the tongue is at the roof of the mouth, the qi should be above the navel. Qi and mind are related. As one thinks of the moving qi, the qi follows.

For beginners, it is helpful to trace the circular movement around the navel with the finger. Later, trace the circles without actually touching the body. End the nine turns at the *dantian*.

2. Then, guide the qi up to the *shanzhong* (heart point) and back down to the *dantian*.

From the *dantian*, split the qi into two to move down along the inner part of the thighs, knees, calves, passing under the ankle bone continuing
to the outside corners of the big toes.

From here, imagine the qi crossing over the *yonquan* (center of the soles of the feet), then up the back of the legs to merge at the tip of the tail bone. Guide the qi up along the spinal column to the *dazhui* (the bone at the base of the neck).

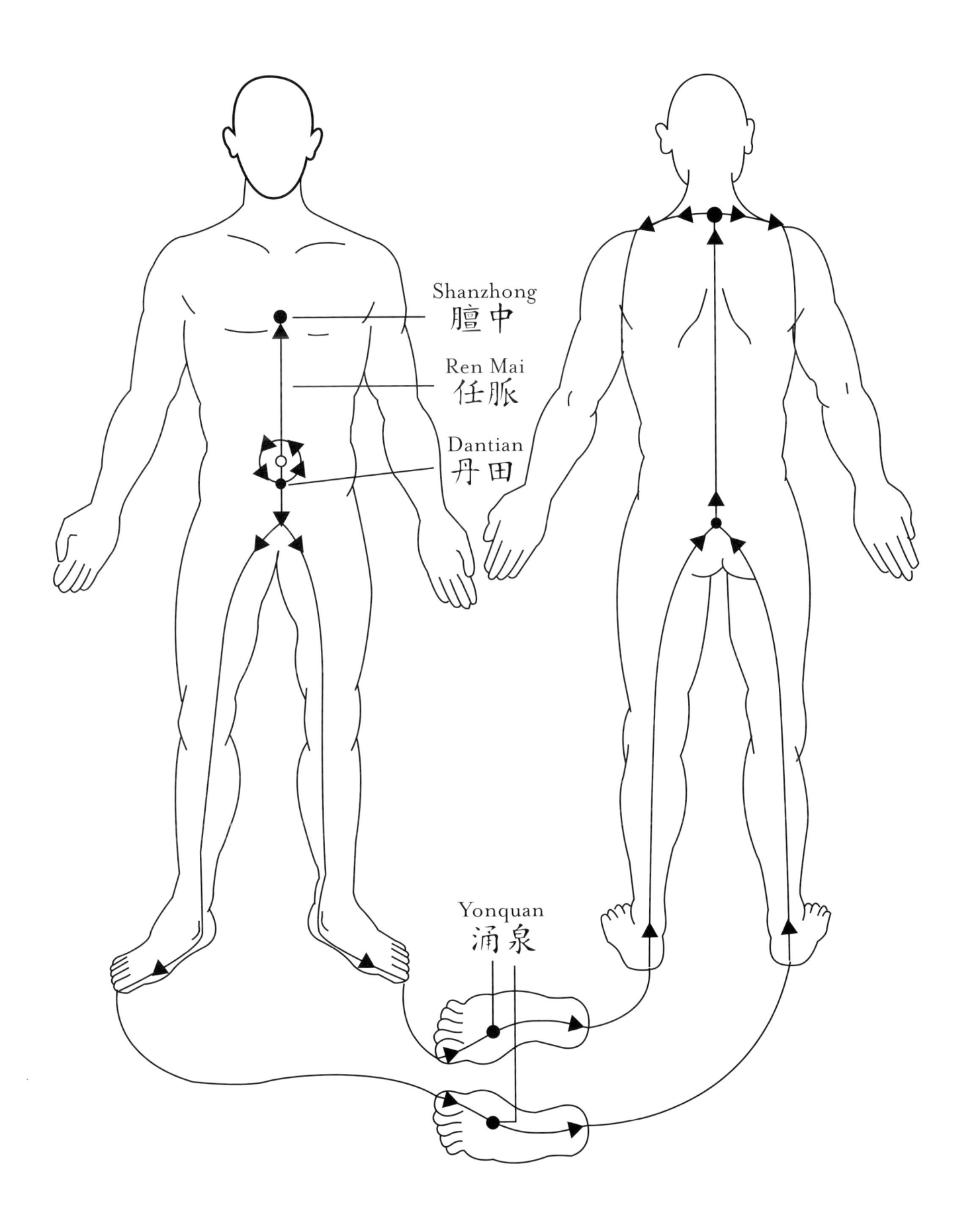

Shanzhong
膻中

Ren Mai
任脈

Dantian
丹田

Yonquan
涌泉

Baihui 百會

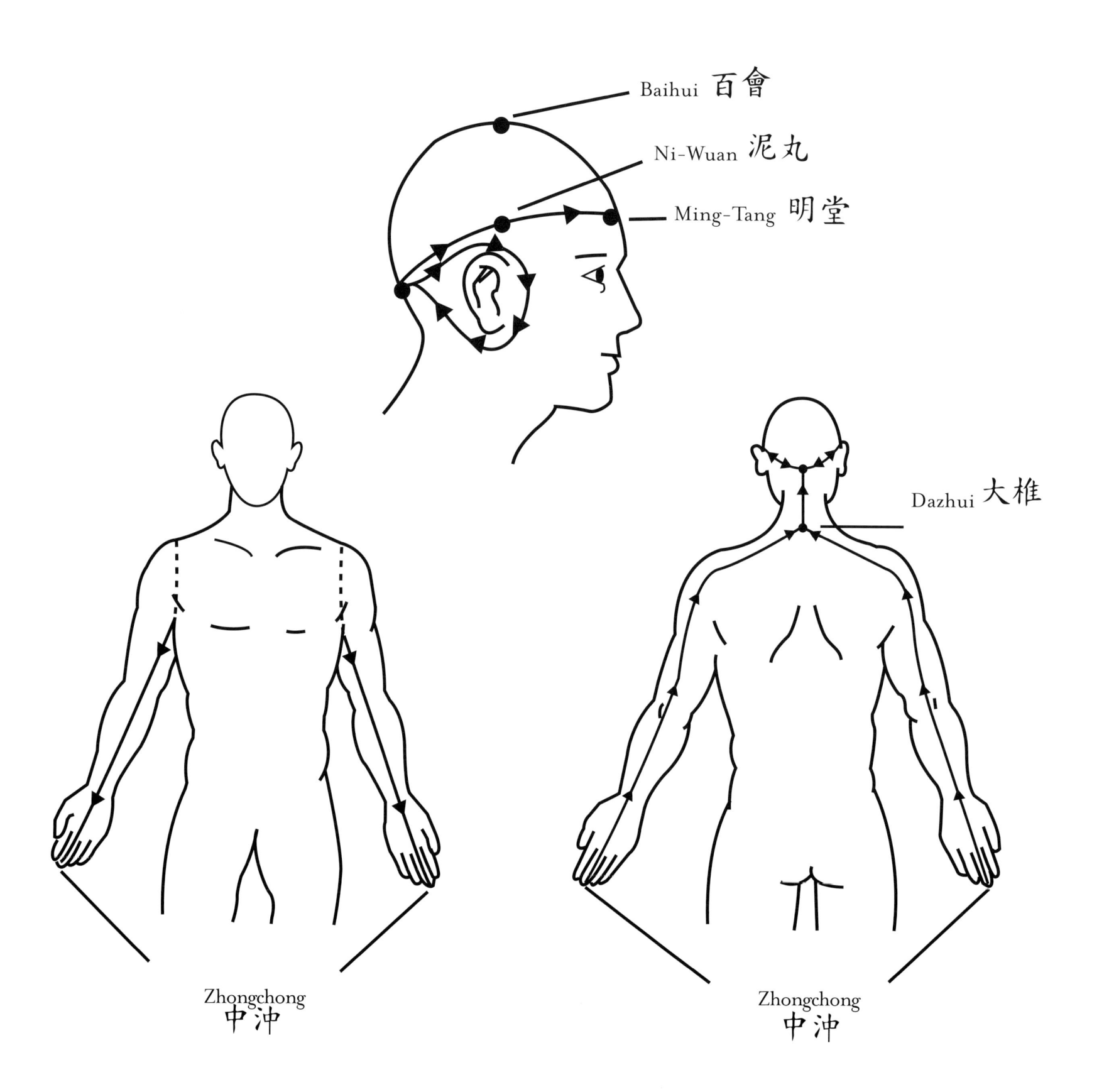

Ni-Wuan 泥丸

Ming-Tang 明堂

Dazhui 大椎

Zhongchong 中沖

Zhongchong 中沖

3. From the *dazhui*, split the qi into two: move it towards and through the shoulders, out the underarms, down the inner side of the arms, across the palms of the hands towards the *zhongchong* (tips of the middle fingers). Then move the qi over the fingertips passing along the back of the hands, up past the elbows, the upper arms, towards the shoulders, to merge again at the *dazhui*.

From the *dazhui*, bring the qi up to the hollow at the base of the skull. From there, again split the qi: move it towards and around the ears and then back to the hollow at the base of the skull.

4. Then imagine the qi go through the head to the *ni-wuan* (point located in the head which is the intersection of lines drawn from the point between the eyebrows and the *baihui* -the center of the crown of the head). Then, the qi goes to the *ming-tang* (the point just behind the forehead, between the eyebrows). Allow qi to remain there a few seconds. Then swallow and imagine the qi moving back down to the *dantian* along the *ren mai* (front center meridian).

This completes the cycle. Repeat from #1 and do as many times as desired.

Points to Remember:

a. This exercise should be done in a relaxed and unhurried manner. Should thoughts arise, let them go by and bring your attention gently back to the pathway of the qi.

b. For beginners, if it is difficult to do the nine turns around the mouth and the *dantian* simultaneously, then begin by practicing them separately.

c. Moving the qi around the ears may be omitted by beginners. However, it is more beneficial to do this step.

d. The practice of **Jiu Zhuan Zhen Dan** clears the meridians and cures chronic diseases. It is safe to do this even when one is pregnant or during one's monthly period. No limitations to one's diet are required although alcohol consumption should be moderate.

e. This exercise is for balancing the yin and the yang and for better circulation of the blood and qi. For those who feel listless, this practice energizes.

f. One may feel vibrations or sometimes feel light as though floating. This indicates the body is healing itself. Falling asleep during practice may happen. Upon waking up, simply go back to the beginning. In time, the sensation of the qi traveling on the surface of the skin will go deeper and deeper.

g. Always finish the exercise with the qi in the *dantian*.

h. If during practice one forgets where the qi is, do not be frustrated. Simply go back to the start of the cycle.

i. If you wish, you may try to coordinate breathing with the movement of the qi. As the qi moves upward, inhale; as the qi moves downward, exhale. Coordination comes more naturally after one has practiced this for some time.

CONTEMPLATION

The human body is a flame.
Let the qi calm and stop the flames of desire.
Moving the qi is also moving the mind.
Let the mind balance and harmonize the qi in the body.
The fresh, clean qi can flush out the dirty qi.
Consciously release the dirty qi.
Then the body is left with only clean and clear qi.
As the clean qi fills the body, it takes on the shape of the human form.
Pure qi then permeates every pore of the body.

The purpose of the practice of Jiu Zhuan Zhen Dan is to utilize the qi in the body to arrive at enlightened consciousness. In this cleansing process, one's being is uplifted and a deeper understanding of life follows. As you are relaxed and quiet, as the qi becomes concentrated, qi can then circulate gently and lightly to benefit the body. This qigong achieves a purified and focused mind that can become one with the collected qi. If you practice this qigong while understanding its deeper meaning, nothing can afflict you. With accumulated qi, you will experience good health, a good disposition, and a sense of perfect well-being in your life.

fig. 1

KUAN YIN SITTING QIGONG

Each and every movement in this qigong is unique. One movement begins with the ending of the previous one. From start to finish, the movements become increasingly complex and require a deeper understanding as one progresses into the next movement. Each movement has a corresponding meaning. It is important to grasp the meaning of the previous movement to understand the significance of the next. This qigong elevates one's consciousness to a transcendent realm. This is the primary purpose of **Kuan Yin Sitting Qigong**.

These movements have deep and mystical meanings. May your heart come to truly appreciate them. Although not everyone can fully grasp what has been imparted through these movements, may you continue in the practice until they resonate in your heart. As you persevere in your practice, your awareness increases. This leads to a deeper understanding.

Today, the human heart appears to be growing cold. In contrast, never before has so much love been expressed in such beautiful ways. In the seeming darkness, there is always grace in abundance and the light of hope which never fades. It is in this spirit of compassion for the world that this qigong was inspired to be shared with all humanity. It is with this faith in the human spirit that we continue to believe that many will take that first step, go on to accomplish great things, and perfect their humanity.

All throughout, this qigong is guided by the spiritual, the purpose of human life, and one's own will. Beauty and love can awaken one's consciousness. This is the purpose of this set of qigong -- to sustain one in the quest for love and the search for a land of peace and tranquillity. This qigong creates a heavenly environment.

Preparation:

Assume the sitting position **(Fig. 1)** following the Basic Preparation Instructions on page 5. Do the **ZHONGTIAN MOVEMENT** (**see p. 3**).

fig. 2

fig. 3

fig. 4

fig. 5

fig. 6

fig. 7

fig. 8

fig. 9

fig. 10

fig. 11

First Movement: Dragon Flying In The Clouds

1. Imagine and guide the qi from the *dantian* to move up and expand. As the qi goes to the shoulders and arms, begin to inhale and raise the upper arms. As you lift the elbows away from the body, with fingers touching, the hands naturally turn (**Fig. 2**). Keep hands relaxed and limp.

Continue raising the arms till hands are past head level, and gradually change position of hands from back-to-back to face-to-face until fingertips touch and point upward (**Fig. 3**).

2. Begin to exhale, bringing hands down towards chest level (**Fig. 4**). Continue to exhale and to lower the hands, separating palms from the base as elbows spread open to the sides till palms are parallel to the floor (**Fig. 5**).

3. Move torso slightly forward while moving hands to the side and forward, in an arc (**Fig. 6**).

4. Move torso backward while hands continue to move in an arc forward, then inward, toward the torso, as though tracing two circles (**Fig. 7**).

5. Repeat Step 3.

6. Repeat Step 4. Do Steps 3 & 4 many times. Inhale as the torso moves forward; exhale as the body moves backward.

Points to Remember:

a. Let the torso lead the arms.

b. Keep shoulders relaxed.

c. Pay more attention to the wrist movements. In Steps 3 & 4, as hands move forward, relax and let hands hang freely. When hands move backward, gradually and slightly flex wrists.

After doing this movement many times, proceed to Step 7.

Variation on First Movement:

7. Right after bringing the torso and arms forward (**Fig. 8**), turn torso slightly to the left, then to the right, naturally bending right arm and bringing right hand toward the center of torso. Continue moving right hand in an arc, backward, and downward to the right, while flexing wrist. At the same time, move limp left hand forward and upward in an arc to the right (**Fig. 9**).

8. Repeat the movement, but this time turning the other way. Turn head and torso to the left, letting left arm bend naturally and bring left hand toward the center of torso. Continue moving left hand in an arc, backward and downward to the left, while flexing wrist. At the same time, move limp right hand away, forward, and upward in an arc to the left (**Fig. 10**).

9. Turn torso to the right again, as in Step 7, and then to the left, as in Step 8. Repeat many times and proceed to Step 10.

10. Allow one hand to catch up and move together with the other. Then, repeat Steps 1 - 4 twice. Then when moving backward, with shoulders relaxed, pull back torso and arms coming to a gradual stop (**Fig. 11**).

Points to Remember:

When turning left and right, relax the waist and let the movement of the body lead the arms and the hands, tracing the circles. The pace may be slow or fast, as long as it is comfortable and natural.

Contemplation

To do this movement, one should be in a cheerful mood so that qi can move freely.

Relax the shoulders. Relax the entire body. Imagine mountains covered with mist and clouds. You cannot tell if it is the mist that surrounds the clouds or of it is the clouds that surround the mist. Visualize yourself going through mountains surrounded by white clouds covered by mist and walking through the clouds.

Lose all sense of yourself. It is as if you no longer existed — as though you had returned to nature -- which is your point of origin. Following its natural path, qi circulates in the body.

Forget all worries. Let go of all thoughts. Think only of the shape of the clouds and forget everything else.

This movement can cure ailments of the shoulders.

fig. 12

Second Movement: Holy Dragon Returning to the Mountains

While keeping the wrists relaxed and limp, slowly raise arms to above head level wider than shoulder-width apart, arms almost straight. At the same time, slowly tilt head back (**Fig. 12**). Hold this position for a while.

Points to Remember:

a. Relax the body keeping the spine erect as you stretch the body upwards. Relax the shoulders.

b. When raising the arms, upper arms lead; the lower arms and hands merely follow.

Contemplation

The mountains are in the clouds and the clouds are in the mountains. Your body is surrounded by a mysterious mist; you cannot recognize anything. It is as though you were unconscious. Sit straight and gently stretch your neck upwards. Feel very stable and very still like you were a big bell sitting on the ground.

You are awakened by the spirit from the heavens and the earth. Letting go your ego, you search for the meaning of life. The true meaning of the Holy Dragon Returning to the Mountains is to return to heaven. Think quietly about how you came to this world; how this world is coming and going. When you do this movement, your mind is in motion although the physical movement has stopped.

fig. 13

fig. 14

fig. 15

fig. 16

fig. 17

Third Movement: Cloudy Mountain Going Through The Mist

1. Slowly tilt body to the right. At the same time, turn the head to face the right hand and allow the arms to drop till hands are at shoulder level. Wrists are relaxed (**Fig. 13**).

2. Then, while exhaling, swing torso forward and to the left with left elbow leading and arms following. Gaze gently rests on right hand. The arms should be at the level of the solar plexus. Left palm faces torso (**Fig. 14**). Right elbow should be slightly bent, right palm with wrist flexed, facing out.

3. While inhaling, pull torso slightly backward. Relax and continue sweeping hands to the left; head follows the direction of the hands (**Fig. 15**).

4. Then, while exhaling, swing torso forward and to the right, with right elbow leading and arms following. Gaze gently rests on left hand. At the same time, gradually flex left wrist so that palm now faces out, and slightly bend right wrist so that palm now faces body (**Fig. 16**).

5. Repeat No. 3, this time to the right side. While inhaling, pull torso slightly backward. Relax and continue sweeping hands to the right, head following the direction of the hands (**Fig. 17**).

6. Repeat No. 2.

7. Repeat the movement from one side to the other many times.

Points to Remember:

Expand chest and move in an arc when swinging the torso from side to side. Use the body and its momentum to lead the arms. Movements should be slow and continuous.

Contemplation

All sorrow, like clouds just pass by
Little by little the movement begins,
like clouds, like mist.

The mountain moves, the mist follows
The mist rises, the mountain follows.

The hands move smoothly
like drawing silk out of a cocoon.
Allow the qi to pass through
Left is mountain, right is mist
That is natural.

Heaven guides, and you follow
Is it the mountain or the mist?
Practice, simply try.

The waist follows the bend in the mountain
Your waist is the bend in the mountain
The hands follow as the mist turns
Your hands become the mist.
In the mist is the mountain.

This is the realm of the saints
This is Heaven.

Here, you come to cultivate enlightenment
Here, no worry, no anger, only happiness.

Cultivate yourself within
Deep inside… practice within
Your movement may not be precise
It does not matter.

You start from non-action and move into action. As your body is in continuous motion, your mind reaches a higher level. This movement shows that the world is constantly moving and evolving.

All actions are natural. You are a product of nature and eventually, you will return to nature. What does it mean to return to nature?

It means to return to a world that is pure, perfect, and nurturing. Your heart follows your consciousness. When you reach a blissful state, you let go your negativities and your selfishness. There are no mistakes. Your mind gradually becomes peaceful and filled with joy. The fog begins to clear. It is no longer as dense as before. Now you begin to see the way.

This movement can alleviate diseases of the stomach and spleen. It can also alleviate depression.

fig. 18

fig. 19

fig. 20

fig. 21

fig. 22

fig. 23

Fourth Movement:
Qui Er Gazing At The Moon

1. At the end of the Third Movement (**Fig. 18**), after swinging one last time to the left without stopping, turn torso to the right, sweeping right hand in an arc, first to the left and then to center, to *dantian* area, slightly touching the abdomen. At the same time, move left hand to the side and outward in an arc, palm facing front (**Fig. 19**). As the torso continues to turn to the right, sweep left hand forward to the right, also in an arc. Then turn the torso slightly to the left to face forward, and bring left hand to rest on right hand (**Fig. 20**).

2. Move hands to the sides (**Fig. 21**) and continue moving upward until above head level. Then turn the hands inwards to face the body. Lower your elbows while hands pass front of face until they come to chest level. In one flowing movement, expand the chest, raise elbows (**Fig. 22**) and bring hands to position turning head slowly to face right (**Fig. 23**). Keep elbows slightly bent, shoulders and wrists relaxed. Hold position for a while.

Points to Remember:
Third and Fourth Movements are continuous. One movement flows into the other.

Contemplation

Focus the eye
On the moon in the sky
The heart is still
A healthy body, a healthy spirit.

You understand yourself completely – no regrets
The body is purified and you know what love is
You bring yourself to Heaven
A healthy body, a healthy spirit.

The light from the moon, so beautiful, so clean
Can transform your character, can purify your body
Long illness leads to inactivity
Doing nothing leads to illness.

To understand the spirit of Heaven,
Always gaze at the beautiful moon
Free of worries, your body is healthy
You can then serve others.

Bring your mind to an even higher level. The purpose of gazing at the moon is to examine yourself, and to reflect on your shortcomings and problems. You understand the world's mistakes. You understand the meaning of enlightened Love.

Focus your mind on the yin-tang (the point between the eyebrows). With it, imagine watching the bright full moon far away. Empty yourself of all your emotions – happiness, worry, sadness. Release them all to the moon. This is both a confession and a prayer.

fig. 24　　　　　　　　　　fig. 25　　　　　　　　　　fig. 26

FIFTH MOVEMENT:

THE UNION OF QI WITH HEAVEN

1. Turn torso slightly to the left; allow right arm to naturally follow with elbow straightening and right hand extending to the front and palm gradually facing downwards. At the same time, relax left arm to naturally allow left hand to drop behind. Slightly stroke back of the head (**Fig. 24**).

2. In one sweeping movement, turn the body to the right. At the same time, sweep right hand towards the raised left elbow in an arc, passing over the head meeting the left hand at the back of head (**Fig. 25**).

3. Slide both hands down, bringing them together in front of chest to position, fingers pointing upward (**Fig. 26**).

Points to Remember:

Turn to the left slowly (Step 1), to the right a little faster (Step 2) and slowly again when bringing hands down together (Step 3).

CONTEMPLATION

The hands are drawn together
in prayer pose
Pray, strive
Qi is in the hands,
Full and not full.

Receive qi from the universe
Give time to this practice
Your heart and spirit connect
Qi then spreads to your entire body.

You understand from your heart,
You belong to God
Your spirit is purified
You are awakened.

At this time, answers may come to the questions which arose in the previous movement. When you unite your heart with the universe and nature, you should be able to find the answers.

Now your mind becomes even more peaceful. You are reaching the "state of no eyes, no heart, no mind" - total emptiness. You have completely united yourself with the universe and heaven. All things merge in one point. You have become one with heaven.

fig. 27

fig. 27a

fig. 28

fig. 29

fig. 30

SIXTH MOVEMENT:

HOLDING THE LOTUS AND CROSSING THE OCEAN

1. Slowly extend hands forward and gradually open palms (**Fig. 27**). Begin to turn hands outward (**Fig. 27a**). Arms open to about 45°. Continue to move arms to the sides, keeping elbows slightly bent while continuing to turn palms till they face up. Arms are fully opened. Keep fingers spread apart and hands at shoulder level (**Fig. 28**). Hold this position for a while.

2. Bring hands slowly up in an arc above the head, palms facing the crown of the head, arms forming a circle (**Fig. 29**). Hold this position for a while.

3. Relax the body and turn and push palms to face obliquely up. At the same time, gently tilt head back (**Fig. 30**). Hold this position for a while.

Points to Remember:
Allow sufficient time for each of the three positions.

CONTEMPLATION

Look to the future where new hope lies.

This movement will further enlighten you, enabling you to correct your past and create your future, discovering new directions and making improvements. Gradually learn more and more and be awakened.

The saints forgive your deviations and give you all the love you need. Act from the heart and allow your love to unfold.

Hold the lotus, and cross the ocean. The lotus in each hand points in the direction of purity and love. The ocean beneath you has both hope and suffering. Just as the waves move up and down, so does life. As the waves of hope and suffering overlap in life, they weave together to become your fate.

The ocean here is a metaphor. Its meaning depends on which direction you are moving. Like a lantern, the pure, bright lotus in each hand, shows the way.

fig. 31

Seventh Movement:
Shadow From Buddha's Light

Keeping elbows slightly bent and fingers apart, gradually bring hands downward in an arc to the sides till waist level, palms facing forward (**Fig. 31**). Keeping the torso straight, hold head up, as if suspended from above. Hold position for a while.

Points to Remember:
Keep your shoulders relaxed.

CONTEMPLATION

Buddha's light also means the light from your body.

How can you become a buddha? How can you become what the Buddha symbolizes? How can you embody the Buddha's teachings?

You must first understand what life is. This is the first step that one takes to become a buddha or a saint.

The light of the Buddha also symbolizes the love bestowed by God. Buddha's light shines on you until you are awakened. Align your love with Buddha's heart. In this way, Heaven and you become united as one; you will be granted both power and guidance. This movement implies that you have attained your life's goal and lifetime wish.

At this moment, you have a peaceful mind. After experiencing life's ups and downs, your love is integrated with your body. When you quiet down and practice Buddha's discipline, you master your inner mind. This becomes a new starting point as well as the beginning of an even higher level of awareness.

fig. 32

fig. 33

fig. 34

fig. 35 front

fig. 35 side

fig. 36

fig. 37

Eighth Movement:
Parting The Clouds And Seeing The Sun

1. Gradually turn palms to face down and slowly move hands in an arc -- forward, then inward to front of chest (**Fig. 32**).

2. Bring palms together starting from fingertips to base of hands with fingers pointing up (**Fig. 33**). Then, slowly bend torso forward; keeping palms together so fingers point forward. Turn the hands downwards, gradually opening from the base of palms to face abdomen with hands relaxed and fingers pointing down toward the *dantian* (**Fig. 34**).

3. Slowly extend hands forward with relaxed wrists, as torso continues to bend forward till palms are stretched out and head faces down (**Fig. 35 front & side**).

4. Keeping arms straight, spread open to the sides with palms still facing down (**Fig. 36**). Then, raise torso to upright position while pressing down with palms, keeping elbows slightly bent, hands flexed at sides (**Fig. 37**). Hold this position for a while.

Points to Remember:

All movements must be continuous.

When holding position, keep torso erect and spine straight.

Contemplation

The clouds are just like a mysterious mist -- like human life. To part the mist is to be awakened, to stand on higher ground, and to look at the world beneath you. As you press down upon the kind and beneficial clouds, Buddha's light is on the top of your head.

Through contemplation you have received new inspiration. You now realize that life is nothing but a short journey. One goes through life to train the soul, the body, and one's inborn nature. Now, you stand at an even higher starting point. Look at the world and examine the cycle of human life and death.

Examine your own life in this world. No matter how noisy it may be, no matter how much ugliness may exist in this world, strive to fill your heart with hope and love. Nothing can stop you from loving as long as you keep yourself pure. You and heaven can be united. You will be infinitely empowered.

fig. 38

fig. 39

fig. 40

fig. 41

fig. 42

fig. 43

fig. 44

fig. 45

fig. 46

fig. 47

NINTH MOVEMENT:

BOAT TRAVELLING IN BUDDHA'S OCEAN

1. Tilt head and body to the right while raising right arm, wrist relaxed, till hand is slightly higher than shoulder. At the same time, turn head to face left; left palm facing down (**Fig. 38**).

2. Keeping head facing left with wrist relaxed, bend right elbow, bringing the hand towards the ear (**Fig. 39**).

3 While slowly tilting body to the left, push with right palm downward to the right in an arc close to side of torso continuing out to the side, turning head to face right. Simultaneously, raise left arm leading with wrist relaxed, till hand is slightly higher than the shoulder (**Figs. 40-41**).

4. Bend left elbow and bring hand towards the ear (**Fig. 42**). Then, while slowly tilting body to the right, push with left palm downward to the left in an arc close to side of torso continuing out to the side, turning head to face left. Simultaneously, raise right arm leading with wrist relaxed, till hand is slightly higher than the shoulder (**Figs. 43-44**).

Repeat steps 1 - 4 many times.

5. Gradually make the movements of the arms and torso smaller (**Figs. 45 - 47**) until the body comes to a stop. This position is the same as that in the beginning of this movement, with elbows slightly bent, hands flexed at sides. Hold this position for a while.

Points to Remember:

a. Synchronize arm and torso movements with the breath. As hand approaches the ear, inhale; exhale as palm pushes down. When one is comfortable and relaxed, the breathing comes naturally.

b. Bend extended arm only when hand is at a level slightly higher than shoulder.

Move slowly when bringing the hand toward the ear.

CONTEMPLATION

Welcome to an even higher realm. You have acquired the love which now becomes your foundation. This love can guide you.

Now, you not only work on yourself but also help those near you. This is God's true wish – that you always help others. At this time, you have become almost without thoughts and you have dedicated your body, your soul, your life to help those around you. In truth, when you help others, you are also helping yourself. Gratitude from others together with your own virtue further uplifts you. Through helping others, you continuously awaken and elevate your soul.

Buddha's ocean is also a sorrowful ocean. While doing this movement, you may feel "heavy" in your heart. This is because your mind and soul have become united with Heaven's compassion. Many people seek the wrong solutions in their lives and are often bogged down by their daily lives. Heaven feels for these souls. This is the heavy feeling which you experience in your heart. In the beginning, you may wonder why this is so but as your experience deepens, you will come to understand. It becomes very natural to want to help every single soul in this world with love. We can ease their guilt, help them change their ways, and transform their attitudes.

fig. 48

Tenth Movement: Looking To Heaven And Returning To Oneness

Lift arms with hands and wrists relaxed to head level or slightly higher. At the same time, tilt back head, while keeping arms straight and holding body upright (**Fig. 48**). Hold this position for a while.

Points to Remember:
As you lift your arms, upper arms lead; lower arms and hands just follow.

Contemplation

If you have grasped what has been imparted till this point, your mind will now attain an even deeper level with this movement – a level which is subtler than the subtlest. It becomes an inevitability: All love becomes one. All the people in this world are children of Heaven.

The universe is one. Everything in the Universe is unified in the One. Guilt and hatred are far from love but if you take the guilt and hatred and return them to their point of origin, you will find that there is a fine line between hatred and love. Love can dissolve hatred. With a selfless heart, one has the capacity to forgive oneself and one's lifetime enemy.

There are no assurances that one can arrive at this perfect love. Even then, one strives to reach it. Even if one has gone astray, one can, with a selfless heart, firmly resolve to make the effort to change one's ways.

Imagine being the enemy. Would you not rather be forgiven and loved? If you put yourself in the other's place and were given a little love, it could melt your hatred and dissolve your negativity. It would transform you and bring you to a loving world. Realize that in life, loving and helping others is of supreme importance. Do you think you have the capacity to sacrifice yourself for others? Can you love them enough to give them the opportunity to change for the better?

fig. 49

Eleventh Movement: Returning To The Ninth Level Of Heaven

Gradually bend elbows to bring them down to the sides of the body; palms face forward, fingers are apart while the head turns slightly to the left (**Fig. 49**). Hold this position for a while.

Points to Remember:
Keep body and head upright as if suspended from above. Turn head to the left to a comfortable angle. Hands are wider apart than elbows.

Contemplation

Through the contemplations, may all come to understand Heaven's purpose in imparting this qigong. In time, may all come to the higher world – to experience the world of love, the natural state, and the unconditional love that permeates it. A beautiful world of benevolence and peace will be created.

Through the guidance of this qigong, those who stray learn from the past. Then, that tendency to stray eventually dissolves into nothingness and brings them to the higher world.

The Ninth Level signifies the highest level of attainment in Heaven. Though not all can reach this plane, it is Heaven's wish that everyone does. When you become one with Heaven, this wish also becomes yours.

fig. 50

fig. 51

fig. 52

fig. 53

Twelfth Movement: Rain Shower Of Apricot Blossoms

1. Keeping head facing left, inhale while tilting head and body to the right, extending right arm to the right and the left arm down to the left. Then slightly raise arms with relaxed wrists till right hand is a little higher than shoulder, left hand at about chest level (**Fig. 50**).

2. While exhaling, lower arms gently, elbows first and bending slightly, followed by the wrists, hands pressing down and flexing (**Fig. 51**).

3. While inhaling, raise arms again, as in Step 1 (**Fig. 50**).

4. While exhaling, lower arms again, as in Step 2 (**Fig. 51**).

5. Continue up and down movement of the arms similar to a bird flapping its wings. This time also flutter the fingers slowly at first gradually increasing the tempo. As fingers and arms move faster, up and down movement of the arms become smaller. Twist the torso rhythmically with shoulders, arms, and fingers moving in harmony. Then begin to wiggle toes. Gradually slow down and stop as soon as you begin to feel tired (**Fig. 51**).

6. Tilt head and body to the left while raising left arm upward to the left and lowering right arm to the side. Do these while slowly turning head to face right (**Fig. 52**).

7. Then, move arms up and down twice as in Steps 1 and 2. Continue arm movements, this time fluttering fingers and wiggling toes as done on the other side. Gradually slow down and then stop (**Fig. 53**). Hold this position for a while.

Points to Remember:
Do the movements naturally and gracefully in a relaxed manner. Do not stiffen up while doing this movement. Movement should be rhythmic. While doing the movement, keep your shoulders, arms and fingers relaxed. Smile and forget all worries.

Contemplation

"Rain Shower of Apricot Blossoms" symbolizes happiness. It represents the fully realized happiness you experience when you have become one with Heaven.

Imagine floating in a gentle rain shower and being ecstatic. Or you can imagine yourself like a chirping bird experiencing true happiness and reveling in the lightness of being.

In the midst of happiness, one holds on to the hope that others will arrive there too. The happiness and the hope both come from Heaven. May the gratitude you feel in your heart blossom into an expression of love for God. Acting from a heart singing with gratitude brings one even closer to the Divine.

fig. 54

fig. 55

fig. 56

fig. 57

Thirteenth Movement: Opening And Closing Of Bodhi

1. Slowly bring body back to upright position and face forward. At the same time, move hands to front of chest, facing each other, about head-width apart, keeping shoulders down (**Fig. 54**).

2. Then, while inhaling, move hands to about shoulder-width apart, hands relaxed with wrists slightly bent (**Fig. 55**).

3. While exhaling, move hands back to original position (**Fig. 56**).

4. Repeat Steps 2 and 3 many times and end with Step 3 (**Fig. 57**).

Points to Remember:

a. The essence of this movement is a feeling of expansion and contraction from the center of the chest.

b. While opening, inhale; while closing, exhale. The pace should be natural.

Contemplation

Upon reaching a state of oneness with God, you have become capable of bringing all to Heaven. You have done your best. May your love liberate those near you and enlighten those in darkness. Celebrate, dance as you come to this joyful world!

Opening and Closing of Bodhi is a gesture of prayer. After the celebration, there is greater hope that love can reign forever. If you have reached a supreme state, you will not feel your hands opening and closing while you do this movement. However, you will feel your heart opening and closing and the sensation of life as you continuously give your love. May your actions inspire the souls nearest you.

Bodhi symbolizes holiness, unselfishness, sanctity, and dignity. Like the name of this movement – "Opening and Closing of Bodhi", your mind pulsates with these virtues. This can take you to the highest level of existence. If your mind has reached the state it has longed for while doing this movement, then you have united with God and you embody Love.

Your way of being reflects your mind and your soul. Life and fate are full of ups and downs. Life and death happen all the time. Along life's journey, there are things that encourage you and give you hope. On the other hand, there are things that discourage you and make you feel that life is full of despair and pain.

At this moment, become aware that with your love, you can eliminate all darkness, ruthlessness, and depression. Like using warm water to melt ice, use your love to erase any inequity in this world. Use your deeds to rewrite humanity's sordid history – the tainted record of the past.

fig. 58

fig. 59

fig. 60

fig. 61

fig. 62

Fourteenth Movement: Qi Returns To One

1. Lift elbows slightly keeping wrists relaxed (**Fig. 58**).
2. Bring down hands to front of the *dantian*, right hand touching the abdomen, left hand on top of right, *laogong* to *laogong* (center of the palms aligned) (**Fig. 59**).
3. Bring hands to circle slowly around navel, going up half a circle to the right, and then going down the other half circle to the left. When hands are going up and while inhaling, tilt torso slightly to the left and slowly turn head to the right. When hands are going down and while exhaling, tilt torso slightly to the right and slowly turn head to the left (**Figs. 60 - 61**). Move hands around the navel many times and stop at *dantian*, head and torso facing front (**Fig. 62**).

Points to Remember:
a. Right palm lightly touches the abdomen while circling the navel.
b. Beginners may find it easier at the start to just focus on the movement of the hands.

Contemplation

After completing all the previous movements, we are now coming to the closing. This movement enables you to experience total and unchanging love, unaffected by the agonies and joys in life. Your state of consciousness and love will remain forever pure. Forever!

It is not easy to seek the Truth in this world. As long as you meditate peacefully, let go of mundane and selfish thoughts; remember to cultivate your consciousness; remember to do good; then you will find the Truth. Every person who experiences the Truth finds the meaning of life. Many people have given up the search, which they consider to be hypocritical. It would be foolish to do this. People have become more and more confused. They are unable to distinguish between right and wrong, since many are too busy pursuing fame, material wealth, and momentary pleasures. What is true happiness? If one considers it to be the attainment of what is pleasurable, they are in delusion. But if one has a loving heart, then no matter how poor one may be, there will be everlasting happiness and peace.

The true purpose of life is to continuously advance, endlessly explore, and seek the true goal. In so doing, you enrich your loving heart and are given the grace to overcome all difficulties, both inner and outer.

If you think you have found the true meaning of life, do not stop seeking.

Do not be distracted by disturbances around you. You must go on. When your soul has become strong and your problems have dissolved, you will recall these words which may be simple but will resonate within you.

If each movement is performed from the heart, you will acquire a deep understanding, and your movements will be natural. Experiencing the essence of this qigong lies in how much appreciation there is of its true meaning. It not only improves your health, but also cultivates your soul to become more noble, pure, and generous. Ultimately, you will arrive at an elevated state.

Now, pause for a moment, open your heart to inspiration and awaken. In this is the essence of this movement.

fig. 63   fig. 63a

Fifteenth Movement: Rising and Descending

1. While inhaling, bring up hands from *dantian* to chest level (**Fig. 63**).
2. While exhaling, move down hands back to *dantian* (**Fig. 63a**). Repeat several times.

Points to Remember:
When doing this movement, keep hands lightly touching the torso to help move the qi along the center meridian. Coordinate breathing and hand movements.

Contemplation

Your mind is now peaceful and your body is full of love. Having united with Heaven, you must now forget even Heaven. You have only love – warm and nurturing love. It gives you unlimited power, unlimited hope. You are bathed in unlimited love and hope.

This movement comes from your heart, which rises and descends naturally. Like the movement of the heart, you return to your natural state – the original perfection of man. The natural state is the highest level in the world. It is the state of a loving heart. After you have acquired that state, whatever you do is always in the flow.

This qigong can be seen as a chronicle of our experiences. At first, we develop a feeling of life; then, we attain the realization of awakening. When we awaken to the true meaning of life, then comes the training. The training is difficult. However, we continually work on ourselves, helping both ourselves and others. In the process, we elevate ourselves. With each step, the process becomes more arduous. Aspiring to acquire an eternally loving heart, we cannot waver.

We can neither be selfish nor hold on to any limited way of thinking. After going through many years of training, we suddenly discover that everything is really simple.

As long as you have love and the willingness to help others, people can receive love from you.

If someone awakens to the true meaning of this world, then you have liberated that one person. This person in turn, liberates others. In this way, the world will be filled with more and more love.

Consequently, we are then rewarded with even more love from Heaven. In the end, everyone will become a saint, Tao, and buddha.

fig. 64

SIXTEENTH MOVEMENT:

GATHERING QI

1. Hold this last position for some time (**Fig. 64**).
2. Conclude with the ZHONGTIAN MOVEMENT (see p. 3).

CONTEMPLATION

Bring your mind back to the real world. Breathe naturally and slowly recover yourself. Now, you return to where you began but the awakening that you experienced remains.

From your new state of consciousness, you guide your actions. For instance, you may have doubted your ability to help a friend but after performing these movements, you will now know where to start.

Having united with Heaven, you are given a new beginning. Your mind has become peaceful and you will find the answer. Now, according to your ability, you can help others.

Before doing this qigong, you may have had an unclear soul and a confused mind. This was the state described in the first movement. But now, you are awakening. Although you might only have been seeking the answers to this confused world, you have elevated your being in the process.

This happens step by step. If you can use the principles of this qigong to guide your actions in helping yourself and others, then you are indeed in the process of training your spirit.

fig. 1

KUAN YIN STANDING QIGONG

The practice of **Kuan Yin Standing Qigong** gifts the practitioner with the experience of the sacredness of his body.

As one does the practice, one is physically strengthened and the back is made supple and flexible. The flexibility that one develops in the practice of **Kuan Yin Standing Qigong** does not develop from pushing the body's limits but rather from letting go, from allowing the qi to take over from the will. Through the practice, as the qi flows through the body, it gradually does its work of opening the heart of the practitioner. In so doing, it releases the suppleness and the compassion of the original heart. The grace that is developed in the practice is simply a reflection of the true nature of the human heart -- full of compassion and full of grace. Physically, this practice not only purifies the meridians and strengthens the spine but also helps in developing healthier muscles. It is during relaxation in movement -- not exertion -- that muscles are strengthened.

Become the friend of your body. Learn to love the body. Enjoy the practice and see your body as your boat on your journey to Love.

Preparation:

Assume the standing position (**Fig. 1**) following the Basic Preparation Instructions on page 5. Do the **ZHONGTIAN MOVEMENT** (**see p. 3**).

fig. 2   fig. 3

First Movement:
Boat Rowing In The Stream Of Air

1. Slowly bring weight of body slightly forward bending torso to about 30° - 45°, gradually bending knees, hips stretching backwards and downwards. At the same time, gradually lift arms forward and upward in an arc, to the level of the chest, hands about shoulder width apart following with the momentum. Keep hands relaxed and arms almost straight (**Fig. 2**).

2. Gradually straighten legs, gently pushing the hips forward as the body moves up to upright position. At the same time, gently pushing down with the palms, move arms back down to the sides of the body. Then, straighten wrists naturally when arms reach sides of body (**Fig. 3**).

3. Bend knees and body again while lifting arms as in Step 1. Head may naturally turn left or right while doing this. Then bring the body back to an upright position as in Step 2, bringing the head back to starting position. Do this movement many times.

Points to Remember:

a. Use momentum of the body to lead arms forward and backward.

b. Inhale while bending forward. Exhale while bringing the body to an upright position with pelvis leading, moving forward and up. In time, when one is relaxed, breathing and movements become coordinated; the pace and size of movements, comfortable and natural.

c. Smile and be in a joyful state while moving.

Contemplation

This is a very soft and gentle movement. This cultivates virtue and good character. Clouds rise up from the mist. The heart follows the mind. Cheerful thoughts are wandering through the mind. You are carefree and light, as if flying through the clouds.

Life originates from nature. It should be as if you were born and never suffered any pain nor ever had any worry. You are innocent and carefree as a newborn child. Life was given to man to enjoy. In returning to simplicity, in becoming childlike, one can go back to one's true nature, to enjoy under any circumstances, the life that is given. There are seeds of joy planted everywhere in the world.

Lightness of heart is the essence to finding this blessed joy in one's life.

This movement connects heaven and earth and the universe. It draws the qi of the universe into your body through the five energy gateways – the center of the soles of the feet, the center of the palms of the hands, and the crown of the head – to the dantian *(the storehouse of energy below the navel).*

While doing this movement, qi surrounds your entire body and enters it through the skin pores. This movement is good for all kinds of internal diseases.

fig. 4　　fig. 5　　fig. 6　　fig. 7

fig. 8　　fig. 9

fig. 10　　fig. 11　　fig. 12

Second Movement: Travelling Eastward Across The Ocean

1. From last position of the First Movement, with arms by the sides of body (**Fig. 3**), slightly bend knees and sway hips upwards to the right, with the arms following (**Fig. 4**). Lean the torso to the left while bringing both arms towards the right as though forming a letter "C" shifting body weight to the right, supported by the ball of the left foot. At the same time, head turns to face the direction of the right hand (**Fig. 5**).

2. Shift weight to the left in a swaying motion; at the same time swing arms to the left with the left arm leading the right arm. Right hand flexes as it moves to the left until it passes the center, then slowly turns up till both arms form a letter "C", head turning to face the direction of left hand (**Figs. 6 -7**).

3. Do the same movement as in Step 2, this time to the right (**Figs. 8 - 9**). Repeat the movement many times

4. To end this movement, gradually decrease the range of body and arm movements, swaying hips less, and gradually lowering arms (**Figs. 10 - 11**) until the body comes to a stop with hands at the sides (**Fig. 12**).

Points to Remember:

a. As the arms sway upward, inhale. As the arms come down, exhale.

b. Body and shoulders lead, arms and hands follow, tracing almost a full circle.

c. When head turns from left to right (and vice versa), keep the chin up.

d. Move smoothly and evenly. Sway hips gracefully, allowing the spine to bend.

e. As arm begins to swing to the other side, lead with upper arm, followed by the elbow, lower arm, and then hand, the other arm following naturally to form a "C".

Contemplation

This movement stimulates a person's spirit of adventure and feeling of openness to what the world and life has to offer. Tell yourself, "I embrace the qi and hold it in my arms. Then the qi will enter into my dantian." You give to the universe and you receive from the universe. The giving and the receiving produces new energy that increasingly stimulates the opening of the heart so that one can enjoy the adventure being offered. Traveling eastward means journeying to Love, traveling to the Light, and going into one's own heart. It is that for which you have always naturally yearned.

At the end of this movement, move your attention to your dantian stimulating the qi to naturally return to it. The qi then floats and circles around the dantian.

fig. 13 fig. 14 fig. 15 fig. 16

THIRD MOVEMENT:
PRAYING TO HEAVEN TO SHOW THE WAY

1. From the sides of the body, begin to raise arms, bringing hands together with fingers touching in front of the body (**Fig. 13**). With palms together, raise arms further up and backward in an arc, while inhaling and tilting back the head.

2. Then, while exhaling, bend elbows to slowly bring hands toward the face until thumbs touch forehead. Stay in this position for a few seconds while holding your breath or breathing naturally.

3. With hands still touching forehead, dip back a little further (**Fig. 14**) and then bring back torso to upright position (**Fig. 15**).

4. Bring hands down passing the level of the heart and gradually part to bring to sides of the body (**Fig. 16**).

Points to Remember:
Be careful not to strain when bending backwards.

CONTEMPLATION

After completing the two previous movements, the qi has returned to the **dantian**. *The qi collected in the* **dantian** *from the previous movements then spreads to the body by following the flow of the movement. As the head is tilted backwards, the qi floats up to the* **ming-tang** - *the area behind the point between the eyebrows. This qi provides the avenue to merging with Heaven. Then pause briefly and hold your breath while becoming aware of your head. Bring the "mind into your head," so to speak. Then return to upright position.*

The purpose of this movement is to collect and store the qi in the body.

In Praying to Heaven to Show the Way, one is truly praying to Sheng Zhen in the heart to allow it to guide one's way through life.

fig. 17　　　fig. 18　　　fig. 19

Fourth Movement: Expelling Unhealthy Qi

1. While inhaling, bend knees and widen stance by doing small heel and toe movements ending with toes facing in and heels pushing out. At the same time, raise bent elbows with relaxed wrists close to the body to front of shoulders (**Fig. 17**).

2. Then while exhaling, slowly flex hands and push palms forward till arms are almost straight, with fingers spread apart and relaxed (**Fig. 18**). In this position, imagine expelling unhealthy qi from the center of the palms.

3. Keeping the stance, pull back arms to position while inhaling as shown in **Fig. 17**.

4. Repeat Step 2.

5. Maintaining the position as shown in **Fig. 18**, breathe deeply through the nose (exhale using the abdominal muscles). Inhale while relaxing the wrists; exhale while gently flexing wrists. Repeat several times, at first slowly taking long, deep breaths and gradually shortening the breath, inhaling and exhaling a little faster each time.

6. To end this movement, inhale once more and relax the wrists; then exhale and bring down arms while straightening knees and moving feet back to shoulder-width distance (**Fig. 19**).

Points to Remember:

a. When exhaling, imagine unhealthy qi coming out of the body through the *laogong* (center of palms).

b. When inhaling, relax the body; when exhaling, expel unhealthy qi with a little force.

c. Inhale and exhale through the nose, not through the mouth.

d. The pace of the breathing should be natural and comfortable. It is more beneficial though to gradually accelerate the speed of the breathing.

e. Inhale and exhale for about 10 - 15 cycles only. If overdone, healthy qi may also be expelled.

Contemplation

This movement not only expels the qi which negatively affects the physical body but also expels wrong and limited understanding. This movement is best done with not too much will.

There must also be a sense of relaxation in letting the unhealthy qi go. One must not look upon the unhealthy qi with loathing or as something dirty, but rather as that which when released will leave space in the body for fresh qi. The unhealthy qi is only unhealthy depending on the circumstances in which it is found. But as soon as it is released into the universe, it becomes neutral once again.

As the sun rises in the east, all qigong practitioners are basking in the sun.

fig. 20 fig. 21 fig. 22

Fifth Movement:
Qui Er Gazing At The Moon

1. While bending knees, turn head and torso about 45° to the right. At the same time, bend right elbow to bring limp hand upward to center of chest, leading with the wrist. Simultaneously, keeping left arm straight, move hand slightly to the right in front of lower torso (**Fig. 20**).

Then, turn torso to face front, bending knees further, keeping the back straight. At the same time, move right hand forward slightly facing shoulder and bring left hand upward passing the center of torso, wrist relaxed.

Keep head facing right (**Fig. 21**).

2. While gradually straightening knees,

push body up, and slowly extend right arm bringing hand a little higher than shoulder level, palm facing left, elbow slightly bent. At the same time, continue moving left hand up till high above head, wrist still relaxed, fingers pointing down toward the crown keeping elbow bent. Head faces right (**Fig. 22**). Hold this position for a while and imagine gazing at a full moon.

Points to Remember:
Movement should be continuous and fluid. Move with grace and lightness.

Contemplation

Mind brings qi from dantian to shanzhong
Do not stop, move on to the rest of the body
The movement mirrors something –
the movement of the sun, moon, and stars.

Excess yin qi is expelled from the body
The balance of qi in the lungs is improved
Qi floating and travelling the pathways cleans the body.

The light of the sun and moon
have come together in the heart
This is the inner meaning
of Qui Er Gazing at the Moon

Pray for heavenly qi from Kuan Yin's home
And you become nothing
You experience detachment.

With empty mind,
focus on your chest and lungs
Contemplate to solve the questions in your heart

Understand your mind
and you understand the minds of all.
This truth you treasure and keep within.
Facing the moon,
your heart reveals the Self.

Go and roam the heavenly palace within.

Having expelled diseased qi from your body, the qi is now free to travel from the heart through your arms, your hands, all the way to your fingertips. Then qi will flow through your entire body all the way to your feet, to the tips of your toes.

As the light from the heart expands beyond the hands and the feet and into the limitless space of infinity, one is given the experience of the perfection of one's heart. In gazing at the moon, one gazes at the heart and sees the perfect light of the full moon – so enthralling, so soothing, so brilliant. This is the light that exists within every heart that shines forth from an open heart to the universe and back. Remembering that you are the full moon and that the light is always shining from inside of you is enough to bring one to the experience of Sheng Zhen.

After one moves into the transition to the Sixth Movement, one should give oneself time to feel the qi flowing and to savor the light from the experience of the moon, which is the experience of the perfection of one's heart. Do not rush into the next movement. Hold on to the feeling in your heart as you go into the Sixth Movement.

fig. 23 fig. 24 fig. 25 fig. 26 fig. 27 fig. 28 fig. 29 fig. 30 fig. 31

Sixth Movement: Qi Twirling Above The Head

1. Slowly turn left hand to face out while moving down in an arc to the left. At the same time, turn right hand, to face out. Inhale while doing this, turning head to 45° to the left, chin up (**Fig. 23**). And then while exhaling, gradually bring down arms till hands are at hip level, elbows slightly bent, palms facing down (**Fig. 24**). Pause for a moment before proceeding.

2. Slightly bend the knees, turn head and torso to the right, and look up. At the same time, raise arms to the right, above the head, arms almost straight, fingers pointing up (**Fig. 25**). Inhale while moving into this position.

3. Then, bend knees further, and slowly turn torso to the left; following torso movement, keep arms extended upward, palms facing each other, fingers apart with hands much wider than shoulder width apart (**Fig. 26**).

4. Upon turning to face completely to the left, straighten knees to push up body using legs, weight on left leg balanced by right foot while continuing to turn twisting at the waist with arms following (**Fig. 27**).

5. Bend knees once again and turn torso, this time to the right (**Fig. 28**) as in Step 3.

6. Repeat Steps 3 & 4 on both sides many times (**Figs. 29, 30, 31**).

Points to Remember:

a. Do the movements slowly. Movement of the arms is directed by the waist, force coming from the legs. As in a car, the legs are the engine, the waist, the steering wheel, and the body and arms, the body of the car.

b. When raising the arms, stretch them up naturally. Ideally, arms should be straight with the palms facing each other.

Contemplation

As you raise your arms upward, imagine stretching them as far as you can. Between your two hands is an armful of pure qi. The qi surrounds your body and arms and twirls as you move your arms and body. This qi can remove disease and make you healthier. If you have diseases related to qi deficiency, qi is replenished and provides the energy that you need to cure such ailments.

If the yin and yang qi are not balanced, this will balance out excesses and deficiencies. Excess qi will automatically be expelled through your hands.

While twisting from left to right, as the practitioner is aware of the qi flowing into the body from above, there is a feeling of merging with the movement of the qi. The qi moves in a spiral; when one lets go and becomes comfortable with the movement, one feels lighter and lighter.

The significance of the Sixth Movement is that the qi flows effortlessly after one has an experience of his own heart in the previous movement. The qi flows in with ease and expands outwards from the body into the universe.

fig. 32 fig. 33 fig. 34 fig. 34a

fig. 35 fig. 36 fig. 36a fig. 37

fig. 38 fig. 39 fig. 40

Seventh Movement: Building Dan And Cultivating Xing

1. From the last position with hands extended facing left, relax whole body, bend knees, and bring down weight. Arms remain up but relaxed. Bend left elbow, with left hand falling behind the head (**Fig. 32**). Continue to bend knees. Then, turn your torso to the right. Right palm sweeps down to the left cheek and continues to move slowly towards the *dantian*). Simultaneously, bring up the left elbow over and around the head; keep the left hand gently touching the right cheek as it slides down (**Fig. 33**).

2. Continue to move the right hand down passing the *dantian* and begin to straighten the knees. Then turn out right palm to sweep upward in an arc in front of the body. Simultaneously, move left hand brushing down along the *ren mai* (center of the body) to the *dantian*. The knees are now straight (**Fig. 34**).

3. Then bring right hand back towards the face (**Fig. 34a**) in "mouth of the tiger" position. When hand has reached the chin, simultaneously turn out left palm and sweep upward in an arc in front of the body. Slightly twist the torso to the left while doing this (**Fig. 35**). Then move right hand down brushing down along the *ren mai* to the *dantian* as the left hand continues to sweep up towards the face (**Figs. 36, 36a**).

4. Move the left "mouth of the tiger" to the chin and simultaneously turn out right palm to sweep upward in an arc in front of the body (**Fig. 37**). As you turn the torso slightly to the right, move left hand brushing down along the *ren mai* to the *dantian* as the right hand continues to sweep up towards the face (**Fig. 38**).

5. Repeat Steps 3 to 4 several times. To end, when the "mouth of the tiger" is stroking the chin for the last time, the other hand keeps the qi in the dantian and waits for the hand coming down the center of the torso (**Fig. 39**). Together, both hands continue down and come to rest at the sides of the body (**Fig. 40**).

Points to Remember:

a. Palms must lightly stroke the *ren mai* when moving the "mouth of the tiger" downward. Hand does not touch the face but lightly touches the chest.

b. As to the coordination of the movement of hands, the left "mouth of the tiger" should be at the chin as the right hand moves away from below the navel (*dantian*). This movement is like stroking a long beard. The face is happy while doing this movement.

c. Breathing is an important aspect of this movement. As the hand slowly moves towards the face, inhale. As the hand moves towards the *dantian*, exhale.

d. The side-to-side movement of the torso is slow, even, and in harmony with breath, hand and arm. When the right hand moves down, the body turns right. When the left hand moves down, the body turns left. Everything must move in harmony. For beginners, master the hand movements first. Later, begin to practice with the body movements.

Contemplation

With the mind now peaceful, and the yin/yang level in the body balanced, begin the next movement. Breathe lightly. Move your two hands gently, alternately stroking the Ren Mai. As the qi circulates along with the blood, external qi also continuously enters the body.

In the practice of Kuan Yin Standing Qigong, as one strengthens the body, one stimulates the ability to work on one's spirit. When one becomes dedicated to the practice, the body becomes the tool through which one can experience the purification of the heart. Strength and depth of character as well as fullness of being is the result of inviting the qi to come into the body and to fill the dantian. As the qi builds up in this movement, there is a kind of inner courage that is awakened; the courage to work on oneself becomes something very natural to do. With more qi, one develops the inner courage to look within.

The even pace of this movement should be the pace with which one conducts one's life – gently, but not sluggishly nor lazily. The soothing feeling one experiences as the qi flows into the dantian is the power of the love that comes with the qi flowing into the body. It is a direct experience of the qi working in the body, emotions, and heart. As one experiences the soothing quality of the qi in this movement, one develops self-confidence. The self-confidence that the qi brings is a result of the awakened inner courage and strength of character. Do not rush through this movement. It is a movement that can stand on its own. If one is nervous about something, doing this movement has the power to calm you down.

This movement is good for kidney diseases, ailments related to the heart, the relief of chest pains, and other chest-related diseases.

fig. 41

fig. 42

fig. 43

fig. 44

fig. 45

fig. 46

fig. 47

fig. 48

fig. 49

fig. 50

Eighth Movement: Overlooking The Ocean

1. Raise arms slightly out to the side to shoulder level. Arms are kept almost straight, with hands relaxed and limp. Lean body slightly forward; keep chest and abdomen relaxed (**Fig. 41**). Hold this position for a while.

2. Bend elbows, automatically pulling hands back towards the shoulders. At the same time, move feet farther away from each other by doing small heel and toe movements, ending with toes turned in, heels pushed out, knees slightly bent (**Fig. 42**). Then turn palms outwards, flexing hands, while extending arms to the sides until they are by the sides of the body (**Fig. 43**).

3. Raise arms back to shoulder level, palms facing back obliquely while turning head and torso slightly to the right (**Fig. 44**).

4. Keeping arms straight, slowly bring arms down to the center, palms still facing back. When hands are in front of torso, begin to bend elbows to cross arms (right over left) with palms facing obliquely back turning head and torso slightly to the left (**Figs. 45 - 46**).

5. Gradually stretch arms downward uncrossing them in front of body. Then spread them apart to the sides to shoulder level while turning head and torso slightly to the right (**Figs. 47 - 48**).

6. Repeat Steps 4 and 5 many times while alternately crossing the arms, left over right/right over left.

7. To end this movement, from the crossed arms position (**Fig. 49**), turn palms outward, above head level, extending arms to the sides to shoulder level, palms facing out (**Fig. 50**).

Points to Remember:

a. Inhale when spreading arms open, bringing them up to shoulder level. Exhale when bringing arms down to cross.

b. Synchronize turning of head and torso with the crossing and opening movement of the arms.

Contemplation

From the preceding movement, when one is made calm from the flowing qi, one has the courage to look at one's life with detachment and compassion. Raising both arms and holding them up for a few moments is for the purpose of condensing the qi in the dantian. As the waves come and go, and when one sees how natural it is for the ocean to become turbulent and then to become still, one begins to understand that life is like the ocean – immense and mysterious. Its beauty lies in the fact that the ocean, like life, is endlessly fascinating. It is vast, it is deep, it is powerful, yet it is calming.

When arms extend to the sides and swing across the front of the body, imagine yourself immersed in the ocean – which is life. One becomes the waves of the ocean, ever expanding and contracting, yet remaining above it, witnessing its beauty and power. It is only in looking at one's life with dispassion that one can become so immersed as to savor and appreciate the mystery that is life. Imagine your heart as giving and as vast as the ocean, steady in all situations unchanged by the unpredictable waves of life. Value your life and all it brings.

While doing this movement, you do not have to pay attention to how the qi flows through your body. Everything flows naturally. This movement can alleviate diseases caused by weak kidneys, can quiet restless sleep, and stops wet dreams.

fig. 51

fig. 52

fig. 53

fig. 54

fig. 55

Ninth Movement:
Lotus Flower Going Through The Mountains

1. Continuing with the knees bent, sweep hands downward, forward and upward in an arc to cross at chest level, left wrist over right, elbows slightly bent with palms facing the body (**Fig. 51**).

2. Bend elbows in order to bring arms closer to the body. Turn hands inwards towards the chest, then outwards away from the chest in a continuous circular movement. As you bring hands towards the chest, turn head and torso slightly to the left. As you turn hands downward and outward away from the body, turn head and torso back to the center (**Fig. 52 - 54**).

3. Repeat Step 2 many times.

4. To end this movement, extend arms forward with palms turned out and elbows slightly bent (**Fig. 55**)

Points to Remember:

a. Relax the whole body, particularly the chest and abdomen. When hands circle forward, expand abdomen; when hands circle back, contract abdomen. Exhale when circling forward, and inhale when circling back. In time, with continuous practice, the arms will lead the hands.

b. This movement is done in a continuous and fluid motion.

c. As the hands turn in/outwards tracing a wheel in motion, the wrists touch, lightly rolling against each other.

d. Keep your weight in the center with knees slightly bent while twisting the torso from side to center and back.

Contemplation

The circle is the basis of the universe, like the birth-to-death cycle. This movement - - a continuously moving circle- -symbolizes the universe and your life. It symbolizes a healthy state of mind. There is always a way to make yourself think positively. Human beings are continuously evolving; the universe is continuously changing.

The mountains represent the challenges of life. You are the lotus flower remaining untainted and untouched, perfect and pure, floating effortlessly and traveling between the jagged mountains.

As the qi travels through the body, in time, one feels the purity of one's own heart. One comes to understand that even the challenges cannot taint the heart. No matter what happens, the lotus flower remains untouched and perfect.

This movement strengthens the intestines and stomach. The qi massages the muscles and internal organs.

fig. 56

fig. 57

fig. 58 front

fig. 58 side

Tenth Movement: Qi Returns To The Dantian

1. From last position of the Ninth Movement, uncross and extend arms to the sides at shoulder level, elbows slightly bent, palms facing out (**Fig. 56**).

2. Move arms down in an arc bringing hands in front of the *dantian*, fingers apart, palms facing body (**Fig. 57**). Hold position for a while, keeping knees bent.

3. Using forefingers, point to and touch the *dantian*. This is to locate the *dantian*. Then switch to the middle fingers and contract chest and abdomen (**Figs. 58 front & side**).

Points to Remember:

Breathe naturally and lightly.

Contemplation

*Having completed all the movements in sequence, you now have sufficient qi. Bring the qi back to the **dantian**. If you feel that there is an excess of qi in your body and you do not feel comfortable, then you may send the excess qi out through the centers of the soles of your feet. Now, (instead of breathing through your nose) with your mind, breathe through your dantian. Then use your fingers to direct the abdominal qi and to guide it to the **dantian**. This finger movement focuses and moves the qi. First use the index fingers, then change to the middle fingers. The apex of the middle finger (zhongchong) is the intersection of the yin/yang meridians of the heart. This means the qi has reached a balanced level and everything is completed. The circulation of the qi in the body has also been completed.*

fig. 59 fig. 60

The Closing Movement

1. While inhaling, slowly raise and extend arms forward and to the sides to about shoulder level, elbows slightly bent, hands limp (**Fig. 59**).

2. Then while exhaling, slowly bring arms down to sides and straighten knees, to bring up body (**Fig. 60**).

3. Repeat arm movements three to five times, gradually diminishing the size of the movement. To bring to a close, arms come to rest at the sides of body. Stand for a while to balance the qi.

4. Conclude with the **ZHONGTIAN MOVEMENT** (**see p. 3**).

Contemplation

The closing movement is like a flying crane. It is as though one were riding on the crane, rising into the air, bringing one's own qi to reach Heaven. While in the air, one sees nothing but freshly fallen snow – a sea of snow which appears to go on forever. As you land, plant your feet firmly on the ground. Bring your awareness to your feet. Imagine that you stand in a vast, open field covered by snow, surrounded by an endless sea of snow. The field is totally deserted and empty.

There is nothing but light – so clean, so pure. Feel the light that shines out from inside the body and from the outside in. You have returned to the perfection of your true nature.

fig. 1

fig. 2

fig. 3

JESUS SITTING QIGONG

The main purpose of the **Jesus Sitting Qigong** is to celebrate one's humanity and to help one come face to face with the meaning and the power of love. The story of Jesus is an archetype of man's relationship with the divine – the perfect relationship between father and son, lord and master. In the giving of himself totally to the Father, he surrendered his life into his unfolding destiny. The life of Jesus -- his birth, the way he lived, how he died, and the stories surrounding his rising from the dead -- a symbol of how love can turn the death of one's limited self into the glory of merging with the Father.

These events not only explain his life but they also constitute his mission. These events are an embodiment of love. They represent the blessings of God and the ultimate gift of enlightenment from God. All these come together in Jesus. It is not important whether or not these events actually took place. There is much to be learned from what these events represent in the light of one's unfolding life. Jesus was born because of love. He lived and shared his knowledge and wisdom with others only because of love. He died out of love for his father and his fellowmen even without the fullness of understanding. And so, he rose from the dead into the fullness of love, into the perfection of his oneness with the Father.

In total adherence to the will of his Father, he gave his life to serve as the sacrificial lamb of love and truth.

Contemplate your life; reflect on the life of Jesus. In those moments when you love unconditionally, as in the life of Jesus, all the events in your life appear to be blessings from God that lead you to the highest.

If one were open to the lessons that can be learned from his blessed life, then truly, one is accepting a most precious gift from the universe for one's growth and betterment. Learning from the life of Jesus is simply a matter of allowing the spirit of love to fill one's heart and to see that truly, every human being is one with him and what he embodies. More than being a historical figure, the spirit that is Jesus lives knowingly or unknowingly among both Christians and non-Christians. When you lose your way, from inside, he will guide you to the light.

In the practice of **Jesus Sitting Qigong**, one is brought to the experience of that Love – that love from which the universe was created and that Love into which everything dissolves. This is a practice that warms the hearts of all – whatever age, race, or religion. When one is dedicated to the practice of **Jesus Sitting Qigong**, one will gradually be able to hold the positions longer. As you experience the qi and the stillness it brings, you are able to relax into the position and naturally allow the qi to perform its functions. In time you will see that it is the qi and not the muscles of the body, that holds the position in place.

Preparing for **Jesus Sitting Qigong** is a ritual in itself. As one prepares for a special moment, one readies the heart, mind, and body. It is important to let go of all thoughts and concerns of the world, to simply listen to and feel what is around you. Dissolve into your surroundings. In whatever setting you may be doing the practice, do not resist the sounds or the physical sensations. Feel that you are in an ocean of qi and that you are simply merging into everything.

Open your heart to the practice of **Jesus Sitting Qigong**.

Preparation:
Assume the sitting position following the Basic Preparation Instructions on page 5. Do the **ZHONGTIAN MOVEMENT** (see **p. 3**). Then, bring hands to rest lightly on the knees (**Fig. 1**). Hold this position briefly. Gently lift arms as in **Fig. 2** and bring palms together in front of the chest (**Fig. 3**). Hold this position for some time.

fig. 4

fig. 5

First Movement: Love Descends On Me

1. Gradually begin to lift elbows, while keeping fingertips lightly touching as in (**Fig. 4**).

2. Gently raise arms and when hands are above the head, open the arms out to the sides until they come to shoulder level; palms face up, elbows slightly bent, chest open (**Fig. 5**). Hold this position for some time.

Points to Remember:

a. Arm movement in **Fig. 4** to **Fig. 5** is one continuous flow.

b. If shoulders are relaxed, this position can be held for an extended period.

c. For those who do not have the physical strength to hold the arms up, it is enough to imagine doing so. As long as one keeps the chest open and back neck straight, with chin slightly raised, one can experience the openness and the blessings of the movement.

Contemplation

As you open your body to the universe, as you open your heart to the qi and to love, feel yourself expanding, giving love, receiving love.

Expand the chest. Raise the chin slightly and relax the neck and shoulders. Tongue touches the upper palate. Breathe naturally and evenly. Your arms and hands are like wings on your body — long and endless, giving you limitless qi.

The universe offers you unconditional love. You are in the universe and the universe is in you.

As the qi pours into your body, love enters your entire being. Consciously welcome love with your whole heart and mind.

fig. 6

fig. 6a

Second Movement: Unraveling The Heart

Gradually raise arms and move the hands in an arc upward towards each other; let the arms gradually descend so that hands end up in front of the chest about head-width apart (**Fig. 6a**). Hold this position for some time.

Points To Remember:

a. Keep the shoulders relaxed while leaving some space between the arms and torso.
b. Keep the arms in line from fingertips to elbow. Do not bend or flex the wrists.
c. Fingers are straight and spread apart but relaxed.

Contemplation

The fresh, clean qi that has been collected is now circulating in the body. Bring your attention to the heart and feel it expand to the hands. The heart and the hands become one. The hands dissolve into the chest and the chest melts into the heart. Heart, chest, and hands become one. Hold this position for as long as you wish. As you are able to hold this position for a longer period of time, you may notice that your breathing has stopped. It is only because your spirit has merged into your mind and your mind is completely resting in the heart. Relax into that space of weightlessness. Let Love permeate the body to unravel the knots of the heart.

Allow the qi to rise from the dantian; *become aware of where it goes — to the gate of heaven (*ni-wuan*). The* ni-wuan *is below the crown (*baihui*) and behind the third eye (*yin-tang*).*

fig. 7

fig. 8

fig. 9

fig. 10

fig. 11

Third Movement: Supreme Truth

1. While inhaling, relax wrists and gradually move hands slightly out to the sides (**Fig. 7**).

2. While exhaling, continue moving hands out to the sides. Then bring down arms with relaxed hands towards the abdomen and palms facing the *dantian* (**Fig. 8**).

3. While inhaling, bring arms up with the elbows leading the movement; hands hang limp as they move upwards along the *Ren Mai* (center of the torso). The backs of forefingers and middle fingers are slightly touching each other (**Fig. 9**).

4. While continuing to inhale, move the hands above the head and extend the fingers upward; turn the palms to face each other with fingertips touching and pointing up (**Fig. 10**).

5. While exhaling, gradually bring palms together while hands move down to rest in front of the chest (**Fig. 11**). Hold this position for some time.

Points To Remember:
The movements should be fluid; the breathing, natural.

Contemplation

Your heart is full of this mighty love. Your awareness moves from the ni-wuan *to the* dantian *and the qi follows. Similarly, your heart descends to the inner depths. All of humanity and this world is non-existent. You are also part of this nothingness. You are empty in an empty world. Everything ceases to exist. All thoughts are gone. This is the fullness of love, reaching the limit. Everything is included, nothing is included.*

You have become an embodiment of supreme truth. There is only one truth. It is supreme love, unconditional love. When your heart is completely open, when you have become a perfect vessel of love, you come to realize that your body as you know it does not exist; your body is simply that which carries your spirit in this realm. The truth of who you are does not lie in the body. All love is centered in you. The beautiful, the ugly — all extremes are centered in you. You are Love. You are natural. You have returned to the original state. You are Sheng Zhen. In that Love is contained all. In truth nothing exists but Love. There is no yesterday. There is no tomorrow. There is only the fullness of being in the eternal now.

When you awaken, may you think of loving, of helping others, of being an instrument for others' well-being. Remembering that Sheng Zhen is in your heart, may your presence help others walk into their own inner silence.

fig. 12

THE CLOSING MOVEMENT:

1) Gradually move hands apart and bring them down to rest palms on knees
(**Fig. 12**).

2) To conclude, do the **ZHONGTIAN MOVEMENT** (see p. 3)

fig. 1

JESUS STANDING QIGONG

The purpose of practicing **Jesus Standing Qigong** is to experience heaven's power in the body and in one's being. The inherent beauty of the movements draw out the experience of pure love. There is nothing more powerful than the power of unconditional love. It is experienced in compassion, in forgiveness, and in wisdom. And it is also experienced in pure power – in the power that creates, in the power that transforms. One merges into this all-encompassing power in the practice of **Jesus Standing Qigong**.

This qigong is for calming the disposition. A calm disposition has no worries and is able to nurture qi. A calm disposition is empty; it has no cares. Qi is in harmony and the body is in balance. This is the essence of human health. In watching the qi circulate, the mind has no thoughts. When the mind is open, there are no worries. Movement becomes stillness.

This can be practiced at any time but a quiet or tranquil atmosphere is best. If practiced seven times a day, one finds a solution to everything, five times a day, the mind is freed of worries. If practiced three times a day, regularly, the body is kept fit; if once a day, knowledge is obtained gradually.

After one has experienced pure love in one's own heart through Jesus Standing Qigong, expressing love and faith comes naturally. Each individual lives in his own pure world but also lives in the heart and soul of every other person.

This qigong is both moving and non-moving. The physical movements are for cultivating qi. The inner stillness is to bring you back to the heart. When the physical movements have ceased, your heart experiences its original purity. It is then that you are released from your past confusions and difficulties.

Preparation:

Assume the standing position (**Fig. 1**) following the Basic Preparation Instructions on page 5. Do the **ZHONGTIAN MOVEMENT** (**see p. 3**).

fig. 2 fig. 3 fig. 4 fig. 5 front fig. 5 side

fig. 6 fig. 7 fig. 8

First Movement:
Man Obtains Heaven And Its Powers

1. While inhaling, bring arms forward and upwards in an arc, gradually extending fingers to point forward with fingertips slightly touching. At the same time, slowly bend the knees (**Fig. 2**).

2. While exhaling, gradually straighten knees as hands continue to move in an arc towards center of the chest. The palms come together (**Fig. 3**).

3. Continue exhaling. Keep fingers pointing up and slowly move hands down, with the palms parting from the base as they reach the navel. Continue to move hands downward until arms hang comfortably at the sides (**Fig. 4**).

* NOTE: If it is too difficult to sustain the exhalation from the previous position, just breathe naturally.

4. While inhaling, bend torso forward from the hips, locking the knees. At the same time, move hands slightly backwards with palms facing up. Gradually spread arms out to the sides and continue to move them forward while turning the palms to face down. Let them come to rest when they are shoulder-width apart. Hands are slightly lower than shoulder level (**Fig. 5 - front & side**).

5. While exhaling, bring the torso back to an upright position while hands move downward towards front of the body; bring palms to face each other with fingertips lightly touching. Arms are relatively straight (**Fig. 6**).

6. With fingertips still touching and pointing in a downward direction, inhale, slightly bending knees while bringing hands up along the center of torso (**Fig. 7**).

7. While exhaling and slightly bending knees, slowly turn wrists inward bringing hands closer to the upper chest. Palms gradually come together as hands turn upward (**Fig. 8**).

8. Hold this position for some time.

Points To Remember:
Steps 1 - 8 are done in a continuous seamless motion.

Contemplation

The mind is calm when free of the small self. Traveling upwards, it reaches the heavens; downwards, it goes to the earth. All come together in man. The heart becomes peaceful. There is love in the heart. Allow this feeling to envelope you and lead your mind to subdue all fears and anxieties.

fig. 9

fig. 10

fig. 11

fig. 12

fig. 13

fig. 14

fig. 15

fig. 16

fig. 17

fig. 18

Second Movement: Returning To Heaven And Becoming One With Nature

1. From the previous position (**Fig. 8**), inhale and raise both hands above the head extending the arms without straining. Fingertips point up, head tilted slightly back (**Fig. 9**).

2. Slowly turn hands so palms face front as they begin to part slightly to the sides (**Fig. 10**).

3. Torso gradually bends backward as arms extend out to the sides with palms facing down; head tilted back (**Fig. 11**).

4. While exhaling, torso bends forward from the hips and brings the arms with it in a sweeping downward motion. Arms are straight and close to the body with palms facing front (**Fig. 12**).

5. While keeping the knees locked, continue exhaling and bending torso further to about 90° as arms continue to sweep forward. Palms are facing up (**Fig. 13**). As arms come closer to the head, inhale and slowly bring the torso to an upright position as hands continue the sweeping motion upward, extending arms fully above the head (**Fig. 14**).

6. While exhaling, widen your stance. Slowly turn palms to face out while parting arms to the sides as torso bends backward; palms are facing down, chest is open, knees slightly bent (**Fig. 15**). (Be careful not to strain when bending back). Hold this position briefly.

7. Bend torso a little further back while pushing down with the hands and then turn palms upward as torso bounces to an upright position to a more comfortable level. Head remains tilted back, chest is open with the arms outstretched to about head level (**Fig. 16**). Hold this position for a while; breathe naturally.

8. While inhaling, bend torso bringing the body weight slightly forward, letting the arms and the hands follow, coming to rest at head level, slightly wider than shoulder-width. Keep wrists relaxed, elbows slightly bent, head leaning forward (**Fig. 17**).

9. While exhaling gradually bring torso to an upright position as arms come down to rest at the sides. Bring feet closer together, about shoulder-width apart (**Fig. 18**).

Points to Remember:

a. Steps 1-6 (**Figs. 8 - 15**) are done in a continuous sweeping motion.

b. Keep weight of body evenly distributed on both legs, feet parallel to each other and the hips pushed forward for better balance.

c. The width of the stance is adjusted with a heel-toe movement. To widen the stance, move the feet outward by pivoting alternately on the heels and balls of the feet. To bring the feet closer together, reverse this movement (Steps 6 & 9).

d. The degree of bending forward or backward depends on one's own level of comfort. As one progresses with practice, breathing becomes more natural and the flexibility of the body increases.

Contemplation

Qi is directed to the **dantian**. *Naturally relax the entire body. Qi can be stored in the* **dantian** *for a long or short time. The mind follows the qi as it moves from the* **dantian** *upwards, to the chest, to the throat, and to the head to purify the inner self and your body. Qi is then routed back to the* **dantian**.

fig. 19   fig. 20   fig. 21   fig. 22

fig. 23   fig. 24   fig. 24a

Third Movement: Pouring Qi Into The Dantian

1. From the previous position, slowly bring both hands to rest over the solar plexus, left palm on top of right hand (*laogong* over *laogong*) (**Fig. 19**).

2. Bend knees and shift weight to the right, gently lifting left heel, touching the ground lightly with the toes. Simultaneously glide hands up along the *ren mai* (center meridian) towards the chest. Head follows the direction of the body (**Fig. 20**).

3. Slowly glide hands along the *ren mai* down to the *dantian* as weight starts to shift to left leg (**Fig. 21**).

4. Maintain bent knees as weight continues to shift to the left, gently lifting right heel, touching the ground lightly with the toes. At the same time, hands move back up towards the chest. Head continues to follow the direction of the body (**Fig. 22**).

5. Continue to shift weight to right as palms glide down to the *dantian*. Head continues to follow the direction of the body (**Fig. 23**).

6. Continue to shift weight to right as in Step 2 (**Fig. 24**).

7. Repeat Steps 3-6 for some time.

To end movement, glide hands back to the solar plexus as head turns to face front with weight evenly distributed on both legs (**Fig. 24a**).

Points To Remember:

a. All movements should be fluid and natural. As the body shifts weight from side to side, the hands continue to move in harmony with the shifting of weight.

b. Inhale as hands move upward. Exhale as hands move downward. When the body is relaxed, the breathing will follow the natural rhythm of the movement.

c. Throughout the entire movement, the hands (*laogong* over *laogong*) stay in contact with the body, caressing the *Ren Mai* (the center meridian).

Contemplation

Qi moves up and down. Allow the qi to work on your congenital imperfections while maintaining a peaceful, tranquil heart. Try to maintain your focus, guarding against becoming distracted. This movement can release the blocked qi and relieve the feeling of heaviness in the chest. It can relieve stomach ailments.

fig. 25

FOURTH MOVEMENT:
BRINGING ONE TO THE SHORE
OF UNDERSTANDING

With left palm on top of right hand, gently massage the area around the solar plexus. Hands move in a circular pattern following a counter-clockwise direction. Allow the head and arms to follow as the body is naturally moved by the qi (**Fig. 25**). Do this for some time.

To end, the body returns to the center, bringing the movement to a halt.

Points To Remember:

a. It is best that the body and the legs are fully relaxed in order to allow the qi to massage the internal organs.

b. The qi follows the direction of the hands as it moves around the area of the solar plexus.

CONTEMPLATION

The spirit of Jesus Christ understands man's pain. In merging with his spirit one merges with Jesus' compassion. This compassion comes with an unconditional forgiveness that returns all to one. Allow the qi to circulate within your being. Let Heaven's power gift you with the experience of Christ's heart so that you can forgive yourself also. More important than paying tribute to Jesus is understanding the true meaning of unconditional love — for yourself and for others.

Qi follows the movement of the hand as it kneads the abdominal area.

This movement strengthens the kidneys, corrects deficiencies, and removes blockages of qi.

fig. 26

FIFTH MOVEMENT:
CONTEMPLATE AND REFLECT

From the previous position, shift body weight to the right, with the toe of the left foot lightly touching the floor; right knee is slightly bent; left knee is turned outward. Simultaneously, turn head to the right and extend arms out to the sides to about shoulder level.

Elbows are slightly bent with palms slanting upwards from the base **(Fig. 26)**.

Hold this position briefly.

Points To Remember:
Drop the shoulders and relax the arms. Keep head erect like a bird poised for flight.

CONTEMPLATION

One should reflect upon the harmony of heaven and the vastness of earth. They unselfishly give beneficial qi. They give you their essence. You can learn from this by also treating others in a selfless manner.

May you share your blessings of wealth and knowledge to help those who need it.

This is what this movement conveys. It helps to gather qi from the heavens and extract the best from the earth. Both hands are filled with qi; both feet are firmly rooted to the ground.

This movement strengthens the legs. It helps to exercise the upper and lower parts of the body. It alleviates lower back ailments. Do not overexert your back by holding this position too long. You may shift from right to left or vice-versa. You may then take a moment to rest and then continue.

fig. 27

fig. 28

fig. 29

fig. 30

fig. 31

fig. 31a

Sixth Movement: Descending To Earth

1. Move arms downward to waist level while gradually flexing the wrists. Simultaneously, turn torso to the left as left knee turns in to face the front. Left heel remains lifted while toes point out to the side. Head begins to turn left (**Fig. 27**).

2. Continue to push hands down to hip level; keep wrists flexed and point fingers forward. At the same time, swiftly raise left knee toward the waist as head faces fully to the left (**Fig. 28**).

3. Gradually bring left leg down to the ground with heels lifted and toes pointing out to the side. Weight is still on the right leg. At the same time, lift arms to shoulder level with upper arms bent at the elbows. Allow the hands to hang down loosely, keeping them hip-width apart. Head begins to turn toward right side (**Fig. 29**).

4. Bring left heel down and gradually shift weight to the left leg. Relax shoulders and gently drop arms down to waist level. Wrists are flexed with palms facing down (**Fig. 30**). Continue to push hands down to hip level. At the same time, raise right knee swiftly up toward the waist as head begins to turn right (**Fig. 31**).

5. Repeat step 3, but with movements in the opposite direction.

6. Repeat step 4, but with movements in the opposite direction.

7. Repeat several times alternating between left and right.

8. To conclude, lift arms one last time while bringing leg down. Then, bring arms down to hang naturally at the sides (**Fig. 31a**).

Points To Remember:

a. While bringing down the knee, arms move up simultaneously. For beginners, balance may be a bit difficult. In which case, first bring raised leg down, then raise the arms. When one becomes accustomed to the movement, hold balance longer on one leg.

b. Inhalation is gentle and natural as arms are raised. Exhalation and contraction starts gently but becomes faster and forceful when hands push down from waist level to hip level.

Contemplation

The main purpose of this movement is to condense the qi and to keep it in the dantian. This movement must be treated as a whole: the upper and lower parts of the body move in harmony; the left and right sides of the body must be coordinated. When lowering the leg as you raise the hands, the body must be thoroughly relaxed. Qi will flow along with the movement. When the leg and the arms come together, the body contracts and the qi is condensed in the dantian.

This movement can train the qi. It can take in qi through the four limbs and retain it. However, the release and the retention of the qi must be precisely controlled. This movement can relieve ailments of the legs and joints, disorders of the bowels, premature ejaculation, incontinence, and abdominal pains. Doing this exercise will help restore normal functions in elderly people.

The number of times this movement is done depends on individual inclination and capacity. Breathe through the nose. If tired, the pace at which the exercise is done can be slower. The tongue touches the upper palate of the mouth. The movement must be done in a relaxed manner. One should have the disposition like that of a newborn child.

fig. 32　　　　　fig. 33

SEVENTH MOVEMENT:
SHENG ZHEN PURIFIES THE PERSON

1. From the previous position, bring down the raised knee. Soles of feet are planted firmly on the ground and are shoulder-width apart. Weight of body is evenly distributed on both feet. Slowly raise arms up to the sides about shoulder level, as head turns to face the front (**Fig. 32**).

2. Bring the palms together close to the chest, fingers pointing up. Maintain a space between upper arms and sides of the torso (**Fig. 33**). Hold this position for some time.

CONTEMPLATION

Consciously bring the qi to the dantian and then release it to the whole body, then expand it outwards to the world, to the entire universe.

Maintain a tranquil state. Refrain from entertaining distracting thoughts. Let all thoughts drift away.

This movement is for collecting and storing qi. Let qi fill the entire body; let it flow slowly with the blood to all your limbs. In the areas where there is disease and discomfort, keep it there longer. Then, as the qi expands to the whole universe, you experience that you are the universe. Hold the feeling of expansion up to a minute.

At the end of this movement, condense the qi back to the dantian.

fig. 34

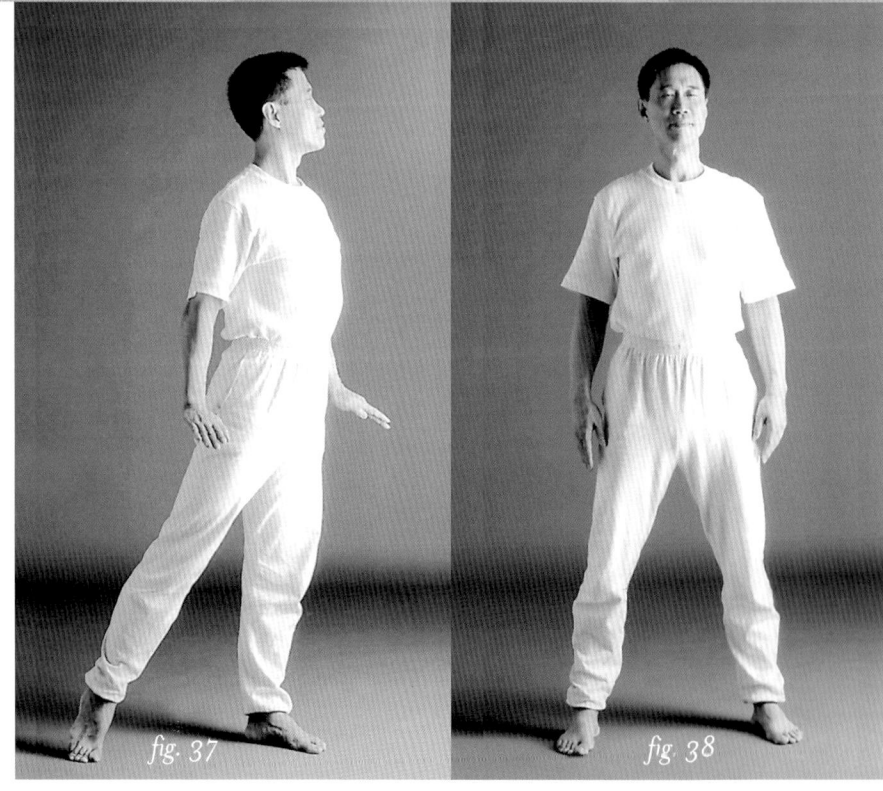

fig. 35

fig. 36

fig. 37

fig. 38

Eighth Movement: The Bridge Of Heaven's River

1. Gradually separate both palms from the base and extend hands out to the sides at a level slightly higher than the shoulders. Hands hang loosely from the wrists. Arms are slightly bent at the elbows (**Fig. 34**).

2. Shift weight to the right leg, lifting the left heel as toe points to the side. At the same time, turn torso and head to the right and flex the wrists as arms drop gently to the sides of the hips (**Fig. 35**).

3. Shift weight to the left and turn torso to the left. While bending the knees, lift arms to the sides with hands above shoulder level as head faces the right (**Fig. 36**).

4. Continue to shift weight fully to the left leg while lifting right heel. At the same time, torso and head turn to the left flexing hands and pressing them downward to the sides of the hips (**Fig. 37**).

5. Repeat step 3, but in the opposite direction.

6. Repeat step 4, but in the opposite direction.

7. Repeat several times alternating between right and left. To conclude, gradually make movements smaller and slow down until body comes to a standstill with arms resting at the sides (**Fig. 38**).

Points to Remember:

a. When raising the arms, inhale and let the elbows lead. While exhaling, let shoulders drop with arms follow downward.

b. Speed of arm movements in an upward or downward motion may vary. Arms may move swiftly upwards and may be brought down slowly.

c. When pressing the hands down, the head and torso turn in unison while keeping the arms and the body aligned on the same plane.

d. The body should feel light and buoyant in order for the arms to move gracefully and with ease.

Contemplation

The Bridge of Heaven's River is Faith -- that which bridges your feelings of limitation to your perfection is your faith. The faith that you receive is a gift from Heaven, a result of your efforts and your yearning to merge with Heaven. Your belief in yourself and Heaven is what connects your small self to the God within you.

When you dedicate yourself to the practice of Jesus Standing Qigong, the movements become more and more effortless. Like the movements which are natural to the body, faith is natural to the human heart. As natural as hope, one is born with faith. When this faith blooms in one's life, it carries you through to the end of your life. It is the bridge that takes you back to where you came from.

This movement is done gently so the qi flows freely. Let your pre-natal qi flow uninterrupted through the four limbs, then to the whole body and finally to the internal organs. Release the stale and diseased qi. Allow the remaining good qi to circulate with the blood to the extremities and to the whole body.

fig. 39

fig. 40

NINTH MOVEMENT:
LOOKING INTO THE DEPTHS
OF ONE'S HEART

1. Bend torso slightly forward shifting body weight towards the balls of the feet. Raise arms forward away from the body to a level above the shoulders. Hands hang loosely down while shoulders remain relaxed. Head is aligned with the axis of the torso (**Fig. 39**).

Hold this position briefly.

2. While contracting the abdomen, gradually bring down arms to hang naturally at the sides (**Fig. 40**).

CONTEMPLATION

This movement is done as though one were looking down from a high place. You see a world of love. Your disposition is peaceful and happy. You are contented with the good you have done. Since all thoughts and actions come from good intentions, there exists no wrongdoing.

The qi inside your body expands. It becomes one with the natural qi.

Your soul is clear and transparent.

You feel as if you could melt into your surroundings. Devote all your love to others: you are the world and the world is you. If you are beautiful, then the world is beautiful. If you are selfish, the world is selfish. Your entire self is the world.

Filled with the power of heaven and with the wisdom of the saints, you look into the depths of your heart. You understand yourself and you appreciate and know all that you are.

fig. 41 fig. 42 fig. 43 fig. 44

Tenth Movement: Looking At Life

1. Bend elbows and slide palms along the sides of torso -- from thighs moving up to waist level, then back down to the sides of thighs (**Figs. 41, 42**).

2. Then naturally bring the back of fingers to touch lightly together and slide hands up along the center of the torso. Keep the wrists relaxed and the hands limp; fingers point downward (**Fig. 43**).

3. Continue to slide hands past the face; extend the arms above the head ending with wrists relaxed, hands hanging freely, palms facing down just above the head. Elbows are slightly bent (**Fig. 44**). Hold this position briefly.

Points To Remember:

All hand movements are flowing and continuous.

Contemplation

If you are healthy, concentrate the qi in the two hands. Direct all the good qi from the top of your head to the heart. There is a feeling of unlimited living energy, of unlimited power, and strength. Let the qi go through the internal organs to the lower legs and back to the dantian. More and more qi from the hands reach the top of the head, then into the body, to the lower legs and back to the dantian. From there it flows again to the palms and to the top of the head. Continue to use your own qi and external qi to replenish your body and energy.

If there is pain in the limbs, you can use qi to remove it. Direct your qi to the painful joints. Imagine natural qi flowing from your two hands along the body to the point of pain.

If you have a headache, you can use this movement repeatedly: Pour your qi down from the center of your palms to the top of your head. Imagine you are receiving more and more living qi to relieve your headache. From your body, let the qi go to the lower limbs then to the soles of your feet to eliminate the pain.

fig. 45　fig. 46　fig. 47　fig. 48

Eleventh Movement:
Showing The Way To Better
The Person

1. While inhaling, extend the hands upward bringing fingertips together and pointing up as head tilts slightly back (**Fig. 45**).

2. While exhaling, bring hands forward and downward to front of the lower abdomen. Arms are fully extended with fingers pointing down and slightly away from the body (**Fig. 46**).

3. With fingers lightly touching and palms slightly open and shoulders relaxed, inhale, slightly bend the knees and pull hands inward and upward in an arc (**Fig. 47**) continuing till hands are folded in front of the chest, fingers pointing up (**Fig. 48**).

Contemplation

As your heart and mind are purified, and as you experience love from practicing your religion, realize the purpose of your existence in this world. Truly understanding love will enable you to live a good life, clean and purify you, and keep you from falling sick. The power of love lights the way; it is one's constant companion on this journey back to the experience of one's perfection.

fig. 49

The Closing Movement:

The palms gradually part from the base as the hands move out to the sides and hang freely. To conclude, do the **ZHONGTIAN MOVEMENT (see p. 3)**.

Contemplation

The practice of Jesus Standing Qigong has the power to gift the practitioner with everything he wishes. Once aligned to this love represented by the spirit of Jesus, everything becomes possible. There is an understanding that comes with the power of love. It leads one to grasping the essence of why Jesus came into the world.

For Christians who want to deepen their understanding of Jesus, the practice serves as a good foundation to understanding one's Christianity and the truth behind what Jesus taught. The fact that he lived so long ago and his message was revealed directly to only a few is no longer an impediment to experiencing what he taught. It is as though he were here right now in the same way he lived among his disciples. He comes to the present moment so that one's experience of Jesus is one's very own and is not colored by others' interpretation and the passage of time. For those of other faiths, who wish to understand Christians doing this practice will allow one to see into their hearts and to feel at one with them.

In time, with regular practice, may your actions become consistent with the experience of the serenity of your mind and the beauty of your soul. Through your efforts, you will alleviate your own infirmities and pain. Subsequently, you will be able to better help others. For the sake of the world and humanity, may you be diligent and dedicated in your practice. Let the purity of your own world bring the experience of pure love to others. May you come to use all your capabilities and all that you have to help those who are in need -- to support this loving society, this loving world.

CONCLUSION

The gifts of Jesus Standing Qigong are endless.

You work on your body and the heart opens. You are gifted with good health; your wishes are granted; and you grow in understanding and compassion for all races and faiths. The more you do this practice, the more you will experience the depths of this form of qigong. It is why it is said that when regularly practiced seven times a day, one finds a solution to everything; five times a day, the mind will have no worries. If regularly practiced three times a day, the body is kept fit; and if once a day, knowledge is attained gradually.

The more you devote yourself to the practice, the more you receive of this power that is embodied in unconditional love. As you surrender to this practice, you experience this power in your very being and in your everyday life.

A spirit takes flesh for only one reason: to manifest Heaven's power in this earthly realm. This power comes to life in the form of Love in the process of blooming and in full bloom. The setting, the circumstances, the manner of unfolding in the human being, are as complex and as varied as the limitless colors of the rainbow. The power which is Love makes itself evident not only in the love that manifests in relationships. There is much more to the word that is Love . . . "and the Word was made Flesh". Love is "fleshed out" in a million and one ways: It may come in the form of artistic or athletic talent that calls all to take notice and revel in the mystery of true creativity and genius. Love can come in the form of physical beauty, perfect symmetry, and harmony in something which has the ability to inspire all to behold and admire. This power can manifest in the gift of speech or an innate power to lead. It is experienced in the wit and intelligence of a stand-up comic, the creativity of an investment banker, or the agility of a brilliant lawyer.

This power is experienced in the lives of people who go unnoticed in the world. It can come in the heart of a simple farmer whose gratitude for rain moves him to tears. Love can even be experienced in the joy that one derives from gazing into the eyes of a faithful dog. All these are manifestations of Heaven's power on earth.

Every single person in this realm is given a doorway to experiencing this power. Thereare no exceptions. The significance of one's life to the rest of the world does not matter. The scale and proportion of one's life to the rest of the world matters not to Heaven. Its seeming significance or insignificance is still part of the design intrinsic to the whole. Therefore, there is neither small nor big. Heaven's power fully manifests itself in each and in all. If a simple farmer feels that God has abandoned him in the wake of severe climate changes, it is as Jesus felt while praying in the garden before his crucifixion or on the cross just before his death.

There is no right or wrong in the manner in which this power seemingly weaves in and out of one's life. It is simply the nature of the Divine Play, so to speak. There ought to be neither impatience nor disapproval towards oneself or others and at how this glorious or sometimes subtle power expresses itself magnificently or painfully. It is still that power. It is still Love. It is still Nature. That is why Jesus experienced the range of human emotions for humanity. When human beings feel that it should be this way or that way, they simply express their lack of understanding. This absence of understanding shows a heart that is still in process of blooming or as the sages say, a clay pot that is still not fully baked. Like the ripening of a fruit, there is no short cut to the process. When there is a growing respect for the process and the time it takes, wholehearted acceptance and the surrender to life is not far behind.

At the end, the only choice to be made is not merely to avoid resistance. That is not enough. When one has arrived at non-resistance or surrender, there is still one more step to be made. There is the embracing of life and all it brings. One chooses life. There is the love for the wisdom of Heaven's ways and the recognition and the experience of the Infinite Intelligence that wields this power of Love. One cannot but bow to all that life brings and the myriad colors in which it manifests itself. When this happens, man obtains Heaven and its powers fully.

To become a better person means to become godly. To become a better person means to unleash the dormant powers that lie within one's earthly existence. For man to become what he truly is, he resists nothing and embraces all. Then comes the experience of being Nothing and being All. The experience is complete.

All this is attained through practice. One practices not resisting. Even if it is not yet fully experienced, going through the mental and physical motions of not resisting what life brings develops the strength and the capacity to hold Heaven's power. Sometimes, life brings that which is physically or emotionally difficult; other times what it holds could be dizzyingly glorious from joy and ecstasy. Whatever the case may be, resisting challenging situations and emotions, or running away from them through denial due to fear of conflict or a desire to suppress one's emotions disables and weakens a human being. Doing this starves the heart. However, the practice of acceptance must go hand in hand with one's efforts to overcome the challenges. It is like the supreme challenge of a chronically ill person who accepts his fate and at the same time fully embraces life. It is a delicate balance. Living life fully involves learning to master it.

The embracing of life takes practice as well. It is important to take time to relish morsels of joy and pleasure with neither guilt nor greed. Gratitude is a good balancing tool. When one embraces the roles given by the universe, one is embracing life. This empowers the human being. It is the practicing of enthusiasm that allows the heart to eventually sing naturally on its own. This is Nature at work.

Ultimately, the challenge is in expanding one's depth and breadth of perception and awareness. This leads to the opening of the heart to embrace all. The spiritual practices of all true paths provide the tools for practice. It is why these paths exist.

Every human being's life is a Song of God, a Divine Dance of the Qi - unique and perfect. Some songs require a wide range of notes. Others are beautiful in their simplicity. What is necessary for the story to continue to unfold for each human being is before him and within him. Sometimes, all it takes is a slight inner shift or to take a deep breath, swallow, relax, and to settle into one's space to know that everything is perfect as it is.

fig. 1

MOHAMMED SITTING QIGONG

Mohammed Sitting Qigong gifts you with the experience of spontaneous joy that lives in every human's heart. Many people have forgotten that within them is the source of the deepest joy and that returning to the natural state will enable one to tap into that endless source of joy in the heart.

The complex world we live in has made it difficult for human beings to be their natural selves. It is no longer natural to be able to relax and be at ease. To be under pressure and living at the edge has become the norm. This way of being has cut people off from the source of joy in their hearts. **Mohammed Sitting Qigong** brings one back to that freshness that is everyone's nature. Do this practice with a spirit of openness.

Pause one minute between movements. If you cannot hold for this long, it is all right. However, you must persevere in doing the movements from start to finish. You will definitely reap great benefits. The heart has no thoughts. No mind. It is best to master the movements so one does not have to think of the movements. When practicing this qigong, imagine yourself in a happy, beautiful, harmonious, and perfect world.

Preparation

Assume the sitting position following the Basic Preparation Instructions on page 5. Do the **ZHONGTIAN MOVEMENT** (**see p. 3**). Then, bring hands to rest lightly on the knees (**Fig. 1**).

fig. 2

FIRST MOVEMENT:
BEGINNINGS AND ENDINGS
RETURN TO HEAVEN

Slowly raise arms with wrists relaxed, elbows slightly bent with palms facing torso.

While raising the arms, inhale and slightly tilt head back. Stop raising the arms when they are at an angle to the body and hands are higher than the head. Hands are a little more than shoulder-width apart with palms now facing the head (**Fig. 2**). Hold this position.

Points to Remember:
Breathe naturally when doing this movement.

CONTEMPLATION

Heaven means the highest state. It is the abode where God and the saints exist. It is a paradise of purity and unselfishness. You come from a place with no flaws, no blemish. Even if you have imperfections in your body, you are originally perfect. May you go back to where the highest divinity resides.

The Self is not found
It comes in time through experience
and practice.
The experience of paradise
dimly remembered
Gives rise to unknown yearnings
and makes one reach out
To embrace the Infinite.
It is a gift that unfolds.

fig. 3

Second Movement:
Purifying The Center Of The Heart

With wrists still relaxed, continue to raise arms even further to an almost vertical position. Elbows are slightly bent. Hands are a little wider than head-width apart. Palms are now facing the top of head, forming a canopy.

While raising arms, bring the head back to an upright position (**Fig. 3**). Keeping shoulders relaxed, hold this position while stretching upwards.

Contemplation

Searching for what one does not understand
Not knowing what one seeks –
One hungrily takes in all that life offers.
Look into your innermost being.
Examine your innate as well as your acquired nature; what do you see?
The gateway to Heaven
is the gateway into your heart.

fig. 4

fig. 5

THIRD MOVEMENT:
ENTERING THE HEART

1. While inhaling, slowly turn palms to face each other above the head, stretching torso to a comfortable maximum (**Fig. 4**).
2. Slowly bring hands down (palms still together), past the face to the center of the chest while exhaling (**Fig. 5**). Hold this position.

CONTEMPLATION

You come from perfection. After the complexity and diversity of this life, can you still maintain or return to the perfection of your innate self?
Praying to Heaven for clarity,
   one comes to realize –
That everything life brings
   can only be understood
     in the space of the heart.
Once the gateway is opened,
   one is free to walk into one's heart
     to experience Heaven.
One enters without fear,
   with empty hands,
     without the mask of clothing.

fig. 6

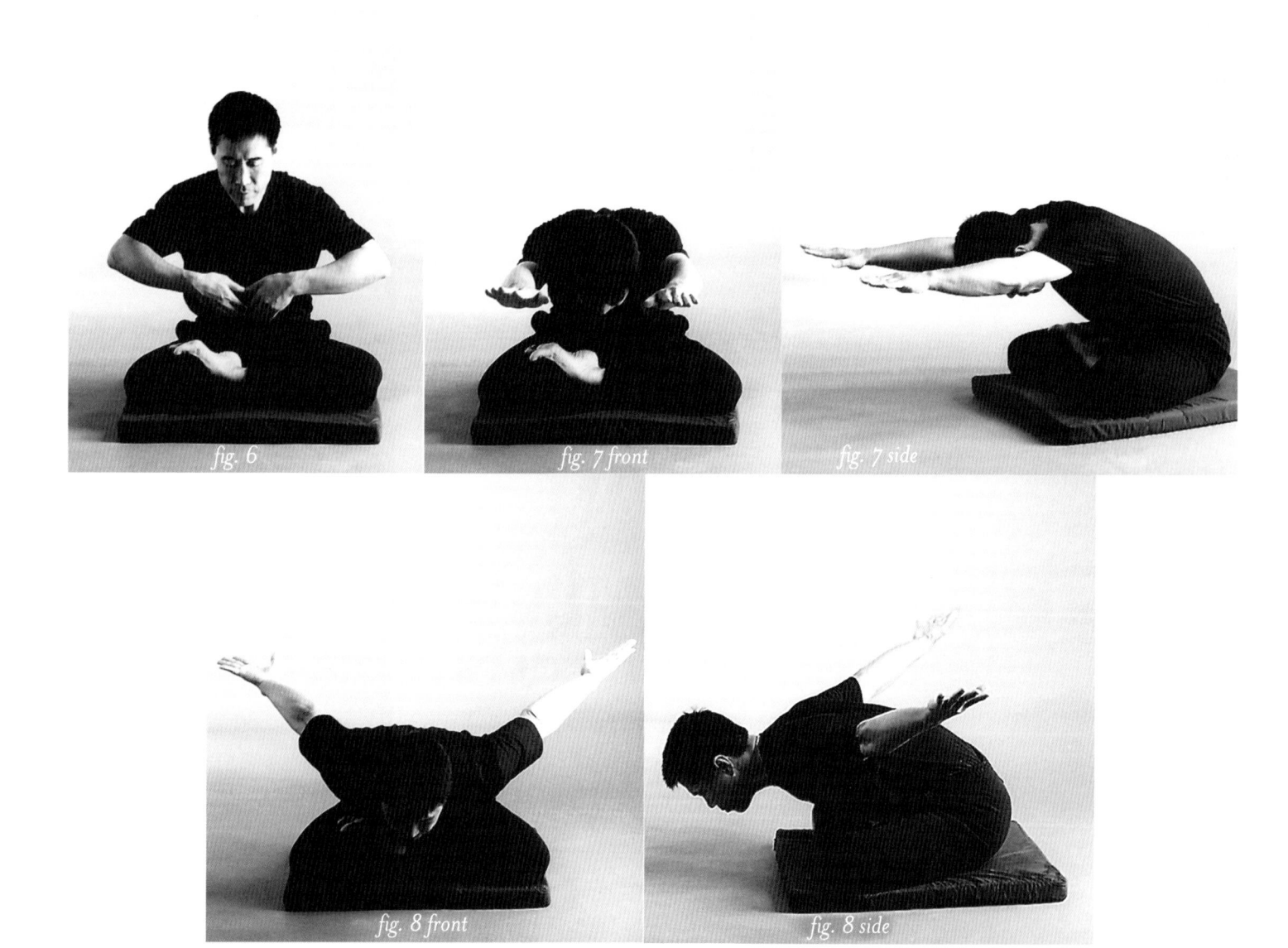

fig. 7 front

fig. 7 side

fig. 8 front

fig. 8 side

FOURTH MOVEMENT:
ATTAINING PURE CONSCIOUSNESS

1. Gradually, bend torso forward and slowly release palms by opening elbows out to the sides and then letting hands bend naturally at the wrists (**Fig. 6**).

2. Continue to bend torso while sweeping hands forward, with wrists relaxed.

3. When to the limit (**Figs. 7 front & side**), flex the wrists, sweep arms apart towards the back turning palms to face up. Spread fingers apart. Stretching torso, keep arms and hands stretched out, forming a wide "V" (**Figs. 8 front & side**).

Hold this position.

Contemplation

*The mind does not yet understand
but the heart knows
That surrender is the only way
to attain the true desire.*

*Held fast in the grasp of Love
and bent low in submission,
One begins to feel the power of Love.*

*It is through Heaven's Love
that one can make the journey into eternity.*

fig. 9

Fifth Movement: Fulfillment

Gradually raise torso and begin to turn palms to face up while lifting arms to above shoulder level. Fingers are spread apart (**Fig. 9**). Slightly tilt head back. Hold this position.

Contemplation

Follow the only truth –
  the offering of Love.
You will then see a helpful, loving
  society reveal itself.
A beautiful world will emerge before
  your eyes.
One no longer strives to take but simply
  opens up,
Accepting all that Love gives –
  unconditionally.
In the Love is the victory.

fig. 10

SIXTH MOVEMENT:
MOVING TOWARDS THE DANTIAN

Gradually raise arms to a vertical position with palms facing each other about shoulder-width apart. While holding arms in this reaching position, stretch upwards keeping shoulders relaxed (**Fig. 10**). Hold this position.

CONTEMPLATION

*You don't know how powerful
   your mind is.
It is a most precious gift from Heaven.
How you act at any given moment
Is determined by the state of your mind.
So you consciously work on yourself
You study and then awaken.*

*Understand that the purpose of this life
Is to reach for and to attain
   the highest experience of love.
At the end even the victory
   is given back to the Lord.
Even the love and happiness
   is returned to God.*

Only then does the journey come full circle.

fig. 11 fig. 12 fig. 13 fig. 14 fig. 15

Seventh Movement: Freeing Oneself To Become A Saint

1. Slowly bend elbows and bring hands down toward each other until base of palms are joined together in front of chest. Fingers are spread apart, forming a lotus flower (**Fig. 11**). Hold this position.

2. Slowly turn head fully to the right (**Fig. 12**), then completely to the left (**Fig. 13**), right again (**Fig. 14**), and back to the center (**Fig. 15**). Hold this position.

Contemplation

The sacredness and contentment that comes from love stems from God's giving and guidance. Everyone has experienced the power of this love. Not everybody can be aware that they are an embodiment of this love at every moment. Not everyone can share this sacred love with others. Let us quietly recall, look, listen, watch, touch, and feel the experience so that we can share it with others.

> *The cage of illusion breaks open*
> *   and one can now see clearly*
> *No matter where one looks,*
> *   there is love and nothing else but love.*
>
> *East is west, north is south,*
> *   all lead to one.*
> *The journey proceeds from any direction;*
> *   One just has to embark on it.*
>
> *The rest follows as the shadow follows the sun.*

To become a saint one is being called to free oneself. To become a saint it does not mean that one will become something that one is not. To become a saint, one releases whatever prevents the spirit from soaring.

fig. 16

Eighth Movement: Walk To The Center Of Heaven

While inhaling, slowly raise lotus-shaped hands. Rest them gently on top of the head while exhaling (**Fig 16**). Hold this position.

Contemplation

The efforts one makes to stay on a course is what propels one along the journey to the final destination. With the effort comes the help from Heaven.

If you see this world as a paradise and see everyone as Allah, as God, as Christ, as Sakyamuni, as Lao Tzu..., and others look at you in the same way, isn't this truly a paradise that you live in?

The cup of the heart overflows with the fullness of love.

There is nothing else one can do but offer everything back to Love.

fig. 17

fig. 18

fig. 19

fig. 20 front

fig. 20 side

fig. 21

fig. 22

fig. 23

fig. 24

Ninth Movement: Stirring The Clouds

1. Release position of the hands by raising wrists and letting fingertips touch. Turn palms to face out spreading arms apart (**Figs. 17, 18, 19**).

2. Gradually bend torso forward bringing the right arm to sweep forward, bending at the wrist until palm faces top of the head, elbow slightly bent. Simultaneous with the movement of the right arm, sweep left arm towards the back with arm almost straight, head turning left (**Fig. 20 front**). Holding this position, flap both hands vigorously. Flap for some time until it comes to a halt (**Fig. 20 side**).

3. Then gradually raise torso to an upright position, letting right arm and hand move up with the body. At the same time, bring left arm out to the side with hand limp, keeping head facing left (**Fig. 21**).

4. Gradually turn palms out with right hand sweeping down (**Fig. 22**). Continue sweeping right arm towards the back, while left arm sweeps forward until palm faces the top of the head while turning to face right (**Fig. 23**). Holding this position, flap both hands vigorously. Flap for some time until it comes to a halt.

5. Then gradually raise torso to an upright position letting left arm and hand move up with the body. At the same time, bring right arm out to the side with hand limp, keeping head facing right (**Fig. 24**).

Points to Remember:

a. Flapping of the hands is vigorous yet relaxed.

b. When torso is in an upright position as in Figs. 21 & 24, stretch torso and raise arm upwards.

Contemplation

Through disciplined and humble service, one is purified.

Through pure and loving action, the embers of love smoldering in the darkness of the world are fanned into a bright flame that spreads over and transforms the world.

The heart is full of happiness.

Think of nothing. Let go.

The drama of life that unfolds along the journey is a play to be watched and enjoyed lightly from the heart.

fig. 25 fig. 26 fig. 27 fig. 28 fig. 29

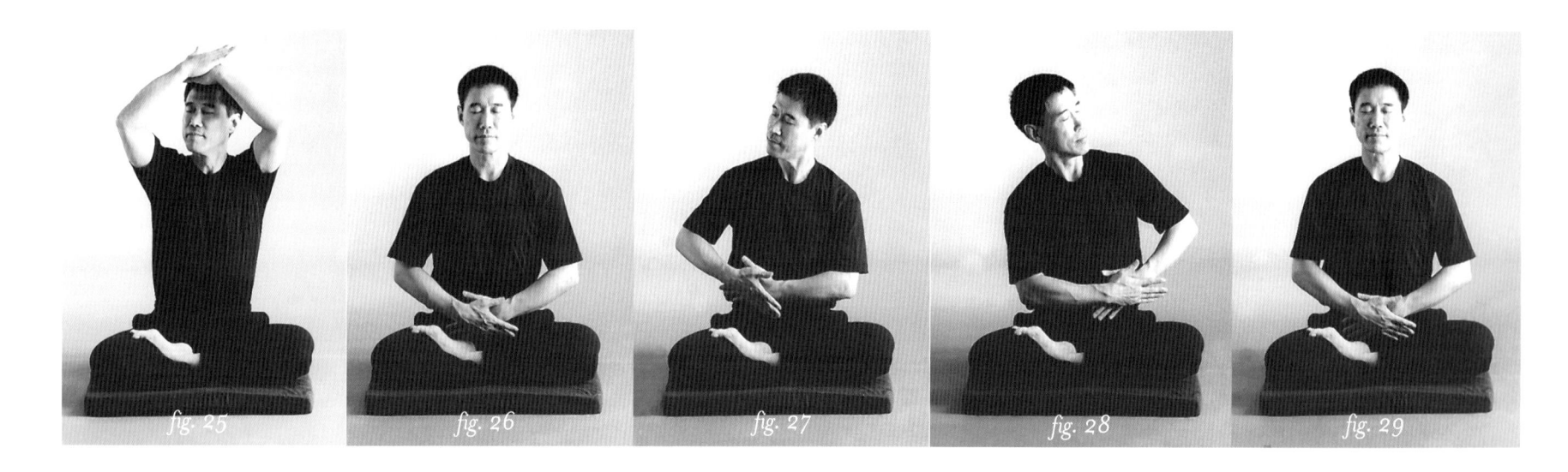

TENTH MOVEMENT:
THE HEART IS CLEAR LIKE WATER

1. From the previous position move hands toward the forehead, crossing right palm over left *(laogong* over *laogong)* (**Fig. 25**). Keeping hands crossed, move hands downward, passing front of face, down the center of torso until they come to rest on the *dantian* (**Fig. 26**).

2. With hands still crossed, move them in a circular motion around the navel (starting by moving up and to the left). Brush palm against the body as if tracing an imaginary circle around the navel. Torso and head move synchronously with each circling movement as follows: when hands circle toward the right, torso leans slightly to the left but head turns to face the right (**Fig. 27**); when hands circle toward the left, torso leans slightly to the right but head turns to face the left (**Fig. 28**). Do this circling movement several times.

3. End the movement with the hands resting on the dantian and the torso erect, head facing front (**Fig. 29**). Hold this position for some time.

Points to Remember:

Keep the head and torso movement fluid and gentle. For beginners, the head and torso do not have to move. Inhale when hands circle toward the right; exhale when hands circle toward the left. With continuous practice, breathing becomes more subtle.

CONTEMPLATION

*Heaven gazes at you with kindness
    and confidence in you
There is only oneness in Heaven's Love
Now, heaven is one with you in that Love
Smiles and tears wash away selfishness
    and impurities
Once again, your heart becomes clear
    like water*

*All journeys end where they begin
From Love you came to manifest love
    in the world
Then you return to the heart of Love
In that truth is found the essence of life.*

fig. 30

The Closing Movement

1. Naturally raise arms to uncross the hands and bring them to rest on the knees (**Fig. 30**).

2. Conclude with the **ZHONGTIAN MOVEMENT** (**see p. 3**).

fig. 1

MOHAMMED STANDING QIGONG

This form of qigong does not require much effort. Movements are natural and free-flowing. Precision is not needed. Do this qigong in the way you are most comfortable. There is no strict way or method.

The heart is empty – no me, no you. Move naturally and instinctively. Let go of inhibitions. Lighten your body to nothingness and fill your heart with love. Your heart is always full of peace and good intentions. When movements are done naturally, the heart is not affected by distractions or emotional conflicts. Think of nothing. Let the mind rest in that space of nothingness. Let go the pain in your heart, the aches in your body. What is important is that your heart is happy. Consciously choose to be happy when doing this qigong.

Practicing this qigong has the power to bring about peace. It removes distinctions between people and reduces conflicts and quarrels. One feels carefree while doing this qigong. Then the experience of peace becomes so natural. This practice has the power to alleviate the heart's depressions. Follow the path of qi and think of nothing. Heaven and earth qi will seep into you and your movements will naturally alleviate your body's and heart's ailments. This practice can alleviate many ailments. Doing the movements in sequence from beginning to end brings beneficial results.

Preparation:

Assume the standing position (**Fig. 1**) following the Basic Preparation Instructions on page 5. Do the **ZHONGTIAN MOVEMENT** (see p. 3).

fig. 2 fig. 3 fig. 4 fig. 5

First Movement:
Truth Unfolds Like A Flower

1. Releasing starting position of hands, bring elbows up till fingers point down and hands are in back-to-back position. While keeping hands touching, bring elbows further up to raise hands along center of torso (**Fig. 2**) passing the head until fingers point up. Turn palms to face out (**Figs. 3, 4**); with arms outstretched, open and sweep hands down to the sides with hands flexed (**Fig. 5**).

Contemplation

Every action performed with or without intention vibrates in the hearts of all, influencing their moods and may even move others positively or negatively. Would it not be ideal for unconditional love from within to govern all your actions?

The experience of Truth manifests in the heart as naturally as the blooming of a flower. It can be neither forced nor rushed; like the qi in the body, it naturally knows how and where it must manifest itself. Truth is a principle and has a life of its own; it cannot be truly explained or experienced at will.

Let your heart experience the Truth as naturally as the body experiences the qi.

fig. 6

fig. 7

fig. 8

fig. 9

fig. 10

fig. 11

fig. 12

fig. 13

fig. 14

fig. 15

Second Movement: Body Leaps To The Lotus

1. Turn head and body slightly to the right as hands and arms relax (**Fig. 6**).

2. Bend knees and shift weight to the left leg while lifting relaxed hand and right arm to stretch out to the side about shoulder level. At the same time, raise left arm with relaxed hand to fold at the elbow, close to left side of head (**Fig. 7**).

3. Shift weight to the right leg to allow left foot to move to widen stance while left hand begins to stroke the head; right knee is bent while the left leg is straight (**Fig. 8**). While shifting to the right, left hand strokes the head in a continuous circular motion as follows: The back of the hand brushes along the nape bringing the elbow up and over the head, down passing the front of the face, allowing the palm to brush the right side of head to the right temple (**Fig. 8**); the fingers of the left hand are now pointing up as the hand stroke the right jaw line downwards, passing the chin, then up the left jaw line towards the nape to begin the second circle (**Fig. 9**).

4. As the left hand completes its first circle around the head, simultaneously shift the weight to the left by bending the left knee and straightening the right leg. While shifting the weight, body and head gradually turn toward the left. As body and head turn, left hand encircles the head a second time (as described in step 3, starting with the back of left hand on the nape) as right hand sweeps down and out in a wide arc on the level of the lower abdomen (**Fig. 10**).

5. After passing across the lower abdomen, right hand sweeps up toward the left while left hand encircles head for the third time. Upon completion of the third circling movement (when the left palm ends on the right jaw line), left palm brushes across the upper chest. As the left palm makes its way towards the inner right arm, right arm is extended completely to the left side, arm straight with palm facing up (**Fig. 11**).

6. Left hand leaves the chest and with palm facing down, the inner edge of left hand begins to slide along the inside of the extended right arm. As left hand slides along, slowly shift weight to the right by bending right knee and straightening left leg. At the same time, turn body and head to the right; allow right arm to be pulled along with palm still facing up. As hands run past each other, left arm continues to extend to the left side while the outer edge of the right hand slides along the inside of the left arm. As the body and head completes the shift to the right, right hand leaves the left arm as right palm brushes across the chest (**Fig. 12**).

7. As body and head complete turning right, right palm leaves the chest and moves up the right jaw line. At the same time, left arm slowly bends back at the elbow leaving the back of left hand to rest on the back waist (**Fig. 13**). Right palm strokes the head in a continuous circular motion as follows: Up the right jaw line, along the nape bringing the elbow up and over the head passing the front of the face; the palm brushes the left side of head, the left temple (**Fig. 14**), then down left jaw line. With fingers pointing upwards, continue to stroke across the chin and up the right jaw line. Repeat the circling movement two more times and end with right palm on the left temple.

8. Right hand then leaves the face; extend arm to the right in one broad sweeping movement. At the same time, head turns up to face the right hand with palm facing down (**Fig. 15**).

Points to Remember:

All movements are continuous and smooth, light and relaxed. Breathing is natural.

Contemplation

Step on the clouds.

Step into the mist.

Go back to where truth exists.

fig. 16 fig. 17 fig. 18 fig. 19

fig. 20 fig. 21 fig. 22

fig. 23 fig. 24 fig. 25

Third Movement:
Floating In A Mist To Truth

1. From the last position (**Fig. 15**), gradually shift weight to the left and turn body and head to face the same direction. As the body turns, right hand sweeps down, left knee bends and the right leg straightens (**Fig. 16**).

2. Continue to shift weight while right hand sweeps across front of torso towards the left. At the same time, lean both torso and head towards the right while both arms move simultaneously to the left; left arm comes from behind to form a "C" with the right arm; look up at left hand. Lean further to the right; flex the ankle, lift toes off the floor while right leg is fully stretched (**Fig. 17**).

3. Simultaneously, bring the body along with arms down to the center; bend knees while shifting weight to the right. Continue to move arms, passing front of the body while shifting weight more to the right, gradually leaning head and body to the left, arms forming a "C"; look up at right hand. Lean further to the left; flex the ankle, lift toes off the floor while left leg is fully stretched (**Figs. 18, 19**).

4. Then, simultaneously, bring the body along with arms down to the center, bending knees while shifting weight to the left. Continue to move arms, passing front of the body while shifting weight more to the left, gradually leaning head and body to the right, arms forming a "C"; look up at left hand. Lean further to the right; flex the ankle, lift toes off the floor while right leg is fully stretched (**Figs. 20, 21**).

5. Repeat alternately several times, swaying from side to side.

6. Enlarge the movements by progressively bending knees more (**Figs. 22, 23, 24, 25**). The movement then becomes more of a "U", like an up and down movement, rather than a swaying movement from left to right. Note that the heel of the extended leg (**Figs. 23 & 25**) is now raised from the floor. The movements gradually become smaller and smaller to make the transition to the next movement.

Points to Remember:

1. The body leads the arms; the arms lead the hands. Inhale when the arms swing up to the side; exhale when arms swing down.

2. When the movements are most exaggerated, the heel is raised. At the start and near the end, as the movements are smaller, point with heel on the floor, raise toes to point upward.

Contemplation

Just be natural. Do whatever feels comfortable. Raise your arms as high or as low as you wish. Your legs may be as far apart as you wish, as you think best. Go wherever you wish to go.

The mist represents grace from Allah, from God; when we are enveloped by that grace, it naturally brings us to where the Truth resides.

Pass through time and space;
Seek the supreme and purest Truth.

fig. 26

fig. 27

fig. 28

fig. 29

fig. 30

Fourth Movement: The Blending Of Qi

1. End the Third Movement with arms and body weight on the left but with hands relaxed (**Fig. 26**); naturally glide into the Fourth Movement.

2. Turn torso and head to the right, with arms following. Arms continue across; before reaching the right side, begin to turn torso and head to face left; naturally extend right arm, with left palm facing down. As body continues to move to the left, gradually turn right palm to face up. Simultaneously, move left palm towards the left (**Fig. 27**).

3. Continue moving right arm to the left; after crossing center of the body, turn torso and head to face right. At the same time, let right arm move down in an arc (until palm faces down) to the right, while turning left palm to face up; then, gradually sweep hand up in an arc to the right, passing head level (**Fig. 28**).

4. Continue moving left arm to the right; after crossing the center of the body, turn torso and head to face left. At the same time, let left arm move down in an arc (until palm faces down) to the left, while turning right palm to face up; then, gradually sweep hand up in an arc to the left, passing head level (**Fig. 29**).

5. Repeat Steps 3 & 4 as many times as desired as though tracing two alternating circles.

6. Gradually make the movements smaller and smaller. End with arms at rest by the sides (**Fig. 30**).

Points to Remember:

a) When one hand is making its way up, the other is coming down.

b) Keep torso relaxed and knees slightly bent throughout the movement.

Contemplation

The form (body) and the formless (consciousness) intermingle.

Relax. Do not allow confusion in your mind, think only of the movements. As soon as you have mastered the movements, do not think even of the movements. Think of nothing.

This movement gathers the qi of heaven and earth. Go back to the original pure self. There is no difference between that which is material and that which is spiritual. There is only that which exists. Truth has no qualities. In this practice, the spirit is elevated to understand the mystery of the form and the formless merging into one.

fig. 31

fig. 32

fig. 33

fig. 34

FIFTH MOVEMENT:
LOVE LIKE THE TRUE LORD

1. Slowly raise both arms forward to chest level; elbows are slightly bent, wrists are relaxed, with palms facing body while gradually widening the stance and bending the knees into the horse stance (like sitting on a horse) (**Fig. 31**).

2. Leading with the wrists, flap the hands in small, gentle movements.

3. Using the horse stance to stabilize the body, twist torso swiftly to the right and back repeatedly. At the same time, flex the right wrist vigorously back and forth in time with the rhythm of the torso twisting back and forth as follows: When the torso twists to the right, the right wrist is released. When the torso twists back center, the right wrist flexes simultaneously with tension. Build up speed and force by twisting the body aggressively in rhythm with the back and forth movement of the right hand, as if fanning a large fire (**Figs. 32, 33**). Allow the bent knees to move naturally as a consequence of the twisting of the torso. Left hand is relaxed.

4. Gradually return to slow, gentle movements, with both hands gently flapping at the end (**Fig. 34**).

Points to Remember:

a) The back and forth flexing of the hand becomes fast, but never too big. The head is upright.

b) Inhale as relaxed hand moves to the right with the torso. Exhale as hand flexes, and as torso moves back.

CONTEMPLATION

The Allah in your heart points not to Mohammed but to the truth of human life and the reason for that truth.

We are called to this life to love with our entire being. Loving like the true Lord means holding nothing back. It is in letting go that we experience our oneness with the true Lord.

fig. 35

fig. 36

fig. 37

fig. 38

fig. 39

fig. 40

fig. 41

fig. 42

Sixth Movement: Fly And Return In Peace

1. While exhaling, turn torso and shift weight slightly to the left. At the same time, with palms facing out, move relaxed wrists toward the center (**Fig. 35**). Then quickly release weight by springing up from the left, shifting weight to the right, bringing left leg closer to the right. While shifting weight to the right, move arms and hands as follows: With wrists relaxed, open arms by suddenly pulling right elbow up and to the side, with right hand relaxed and above shoulder level; at the same time, leading with the heel of the hand, turn left palm to face down, arm sweeping to the side (**Fig. 36**). Hold this position briefly.

2. Bend knees a little more while releasing arms, naturally raising them to a more open position above shoulder level, relaxing wrists to face the torso (**Fig. 37**). Then drop arms gently to the sides and straighten legs with the weight still on the right leg (**Fig. 38**); then gradually shift weight to the center.

3. Bend knees and shift the weight to the left, raising right heel, as torso and head faces slightly to right. At the same time, raise up arms, elbows slightly bent, hands hanging from relaxed wrists (**Fig. 39**).

4. Begin to move pelvis back and forth in the following manner: Bend knees slightly, tilting pelvis back opening the chest, then thrust pelvis forward while torso contracts. Do the contract-and-release movement of the pelvis over and over, slowly at first. As the body builds up speed, allow the rest of the body to follow causing body, arms, and legs to move rhythmically in waves, sending large ripples through the body (**Figs. 40, 41**). Do this for some time before slowing down.

5. To end this movement, shift weight to the center while naturally straightening legs and dropping arms gently to the sides (**Fig. 42**).

Points to Remember:

a. The pelvic movement is quick yet relaxed and natural.

b. Arms, hands and wrists remain relaxed and loose throughout the movement.

Contemplation

What is peace? What is harmony?
It means to express your love
through your actions.
The peaceful love
shining through your actions,
The world will come to own.

fig. 43 fig. 44 fig. 45 fig. 46
fig. 47 fig. 48 fig. 49 fig. 50

Seventh Movement: Man Embodies The Truth

1. Shift weight to the right and slightly bend right knee. While straightening left leg and raising left heel, bring hands with fingers touching and curled up to chest level in front of the shoulders; Elbows are naturally out to the sides (**Fig. 43**).

2. Balancing on right foot, slide left leg toward center, then gradually lift left knee with pointed toes (**Fig. 44**).

3. Keeping weight on the right, drop left leg straightened out to the left while releasing elbows and pushing hands downwards in front of the torso; palms are facing down (**Fig. 45**).

4. Shift weight to the left: bend left knee, straighten right leg and raise right heel. Arms and hands remain in the same pose (**Fig. 46**).

5. Balancing on left foot, slide right leg toward center, then quickly lift right knee with pointed toes. While lifting knee, swiftly bring hands with fingers touching and curled up to chest level in front of the shoulders; elbows are naturally out to the sides (**Fig. 47**). From now on lift knee quickly each time and both sides when you repeat this movement.

6. Repeat alternately several times, stepping from side to side as in **Figs. 45 – 47**.

7. To end this movement, upon dropping the leg for the last time, gently bring down hands with feet apart (**Fig. 48**). Bring hands curled up to chest level elbows out to the sides, this time without any force (**Fig. 49**). Then gently bring down hands to hang naturally by the sides (**Fig. 50**).

Points to Remember:

a) When raising the knee, the movement is swift. When dropping the knee, the movement is slower.

b) Inhale when raising the knee; exhale when dropping the knee.

Contemplation

How swiftly or how slowly you do this movement is not important. You may vary your pace –either slow or fast or both-- depending on how you feel at the time. When you are in a pleasant mood, you can do it slowly. When you are not in such a good disposition, you can do it fast. The pace and the number of repetitions is up to each individual. Man's life has ups and downs. Life sometimes floats; life sometimes sinks. No matter what your stature in life, you are in essence an angel with a loving heart. There are no conditions to loving in this world.

fig. 51　　　　　fig. 52

EIGHTH MOVEMENT:
LIKE WIND, LIKE CLOUDS

1. While inhaling, naturally bend forward at the hips and bend the knees while arms with hands relaxed float up (**Fig. 51**).

2. While exhaling, move back arms down to the sides and gently push down with palms; simultaneously straighten legs by gently pushing the pelvis forward and bringing body to an upright position. Slightly leaning back as hands gently follow the momentum, continue movement.

3. In a continuous flow, repeat steps 1 and 2 several times, with the movements becoming smaller and smaller. End with the body erect and hands resting at the sides (**Fig. 52**).

Points to Remember:

a) At first, the movements are small; bend the body and lift the arms a little. Gradually, the movements become bigger; bend the body further and swing the arms increasingly higher, building up speed and force.

b) As arms float down, hands are flexed.

CONTEMPLATION

Do not force the movements. They must be free-flowing. This movement is for improving the quality of qi and to produce dan *- to be connected to heaven and earth as one.*

Sow the mustard seed of life.
Nourish it.
Allow it to slowly grow, to evolve
    and to be refined into a new life.
The human body is a microcosm
    of the new life
        that will eliminate
            selfishness on earth.

In the same way that wind brings change in nature, and drifting clouds change the weather, man's thoughts and actions have the power to change destiny.

fig. 53

fig. 54

fig. 55

fig. 56

fig. 57

fig. 58

Ninth Movement: Pure Heart Descends

1. Bend both knees and shift weight to the left, leaving right foot weightless with right heel raised. Using the knees as a spring, bounce up and down four times rhythmically while arms swing backward and forward in rhythm with the bounce (**Figs. 53, 54, 55, 56, 57**).
2. Shift weight to the right while raising left heel and repeat movement on the other side.
3. Do this alternately several times, shifting from side to side. End the movement by facing forward, weight in the center, allowing the momentum of the swinging arms to come to a halt on their own.

Hands are now at the sides (**Fig. 58**).

Points to Remember:

How much weight you shift from the left to the right leg depends on the individual. The foot may or may not be lifted. Be natural.

Contemplation

Disperse qi to every cell to enjoy life

The joy of life comes in letting go, in surrendering to nature

One cannot hold happiness because it is in constant motion
One has to ride it.

The experience of a pure heart descends naturally as night turns into day.

fig. 59

fig. 60

TENTH MOVEMENT:
PERCHED ON THE FLYING CRANE

Stand with feet shoulder-width apart. Gently lift arms diagonally to the sides (**Fig. 59**) then slowly drop elbows. As elbows come close to the body (**Fig. 60**), begin to trace circles inward while flexing wrists. As hands approach the body, begin to turn out the elbows to continue with the circles. With relaxed wrists, further open elbows outwards to complete the circle. Do this circling movement several times without stopping.

Points to remember:

a) The two imaginary circles are like large round platters in front of the body.

b) The body is upright throughout this movement.

CONTEMPLATION

Circle the world, go around the universe. No matter what point in time, be it apparent or not, Mohammed's love shines on this splendid world and its people.

May all be blessed with a sense of perfect well-being and harmony. May all maintain the sweetness of a pleasant and quiet state.

fig. 61

fig. 62

fig. 63

fig. 64

fig. 65

fig. 66

fig. 67

The Closing Movement: Love Comes From One

1. On the last circling movement, at the point when the hands have just circled in (**Fig. 61**), simultaneously bend the knees and spring up, by straightening legs while lifting arms out to the sides and upward with relaxed hands.

2. Continue to raise arms even higher. Then turn hands inwards and drop elbows to allow palms of hands with fingers pointing up, to fall close to the face (**Figs. 62, 63**). Glide hands downward, close to the face, along center of the body to the *dantian*. Then, at the *dantian*, let fingertips (which are naturally apart) touch as shown in **Fig. 64**.

3. With knees locked, bend down body to the limit while keeping hand formation at the *dantian* (**Fig. 65**). Then bring down hands as arms stretch out, until hands almost touch the ground.

4. Gradually bring the body back to upright position while lifting outstretched arms upward (**Fig. 66**). Continue raising hands even higher.

5. Bring hands down, palms together, past the face. Stop at the center of the chest (**Fig. 67**).

6. Conclude with the **ZHONGTIAN MOVEMENT** (see p. 3).

Contemplation

Pour qi into the dantian.

Return to the natural.

Both hands come together before the chest.

The heart and consciousness become one.

Love originally comes from One.

CONCLUSION

A life of joy is the gift Mohammed wishes to grant to mankind. A life of joy in loving Allah, in praising Allah is what brings one to that wellspring of joy in the heart of every man. The journey to Mecca is truly a journey into the heart. All human beings are invited to make that journey to the Mecca in their hearts. The peace that all humanity yearns for will come one day but must first be experienced in the heart. When it is experienced in the heart, the natural fruit of this experience is to look at your brother and see what is the same between you and your brother. You will see that in his eyes that he, too, yearns for the peace; he, too, yearns to be able to walk into the Mecca in his heart.

The Mecca in the heart -- the experience of unconditional love within -- the experience of Sheng Zhen.

The aim of Islam is to embrace all and to dissolve all hatred through love. May all people lay down their weapons and use their hearts to eradicate all anguish. Weapons are walls. Only the fire of the heart, love, and understanding can burn down those walls. When you enter into the silence of the heart, Mohammed is in your heart.

No matter what your beliefs are, all in Heaven come together in love as one. At that moment when your heart merges with Heaven, there is a convergence of love. This love contains empathy. This love contains everything. There are seeds of love in everyone. Although some may sow seeds from misguided actions, these deeds really stem from a thirst for love coming from a rigid and inflexible way of seeking the Truth.

Ask your heart. Open your eyes. See that in your hands you hold different choices. May you choose a way that does not cause pain to others. This is the way of love. Only under the power of love can you talk about peace and fraternal love. In that love exists a beautiful world, blue skies, white clouds, birds floating freely in the air, and verdant forests - nature as it was originally. In that world, people encourage and sustain one another in the spirit of helping each other.

The fighting that continues to be waged around the world is a result of the frustration of not being able to experience the peace that everyone yearns for. It is sad that they look towards the wrong direction to acquire that peace. May every human being realize where the true peace is found, sooner rather than later. But it will happen when it is meant to happen. Every human being's main responsibility is truly to himself.

The winds of change will always be there. Everyone must be ready to shift direction at a moment's notice. You may lose your home in an instant. But if you know that your home is your heart, the Mecca in your heart, then the winds of change will have no bearing on your state of being.

Peace will come only when all men truly recognize that every human being on this earth yearns for peace. Differences lie in the manner with which they attempt to attain it.

Through hardships, as you work to solve difficulties, step by step, your spirit grows. Gradually, you come to the center point of consciousness. What is this point? Where is this point? For this, you need to learn, study, and experience.

Sheng Zhen is a precious gift and the pivotal point of all religions, because in the heart of all faiths and paths is unconditional love. Between and among religions, there are no conflicts.

All are manifestations of love. Open your eyes. Look to your left, look to your right. These are your brothers and sisters. Lovingly give them compassion and understanding.

Sheng Zhen is a warm and loving world. How does one come to this world? Whether one follows the original spirit of his religion or one follows the spirit of Sheng Zhen, all can come to this warm, loving world. Everyone can share the sweetness and bliss of this love with others.

Despite the violence, despite the bloodshed, be firm in the conviction that the lovers of the Truth, the sages of all time, the spiritual leaders that have walked the face of the earth gaze upon humanity and love them unceasingly. Trust in the manner in which destiny unfolds.

For now, for your own singular life, look around you. That which is simply natural is glorious. May all seek that which is natural. Enjoy the world that you see - gifts from nature and gifts from your fellowmen. Embrace a piece of sky and throw yourself into Nature. Let go; allow the joy that resides in your heart to sing in all its splendor and trust that the glory of God reigns now, then, and always.

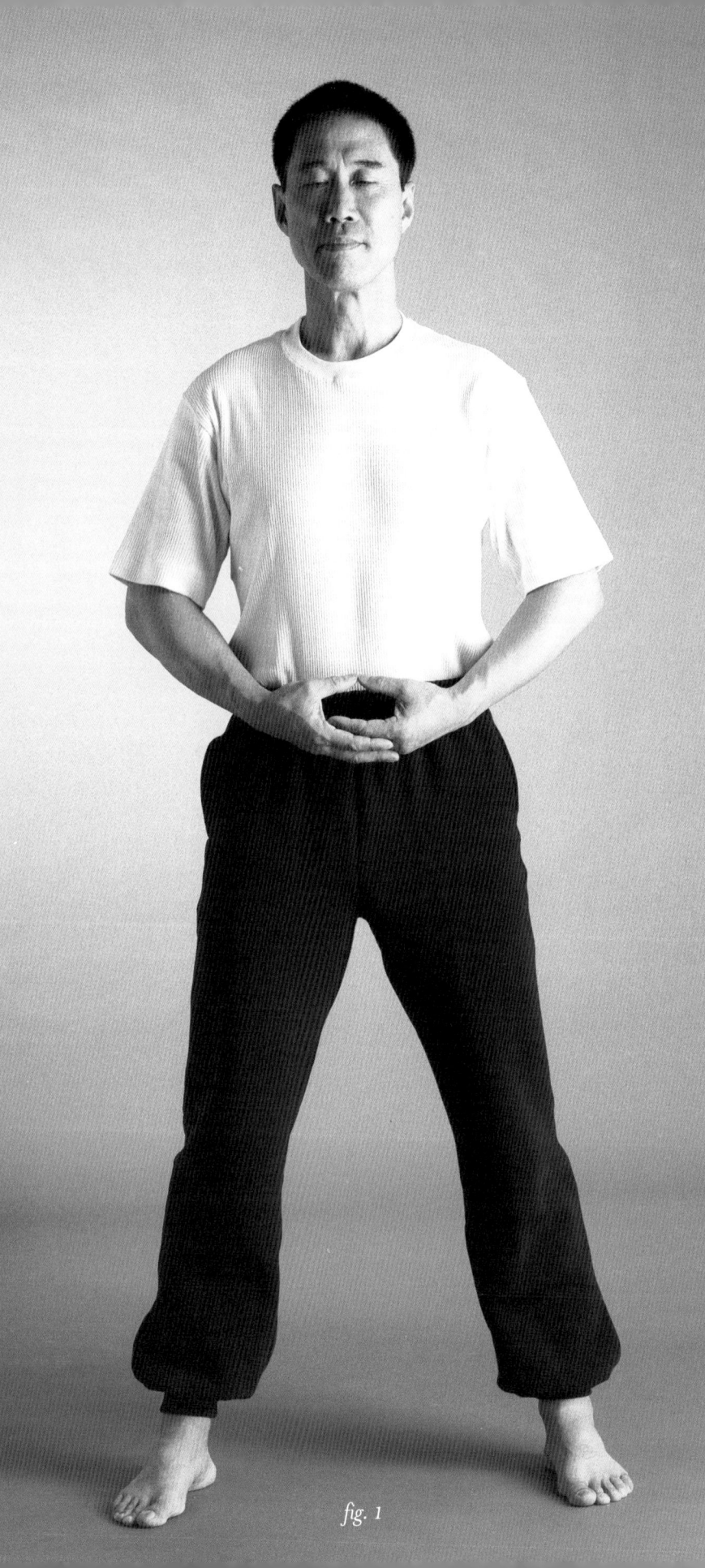

fig. 1

回春一丹功

HUI CHUN YIDAN
RETURN TO SPRING
Inspired by Lao Tzu

A thousand autumns ago, the world was vast.
Ten thousand things need first a way.
Ten thousand li of heaven and earth save mankind.
Drive away worries. Welcome happy events. Play in the heavens.
Thinking not of troubles, forget the self;
Wander freely in nature.

Let the body be at ease.
In any qigong movement, let the body be relaxed.
Go back to spring, return to youth.
Go back to a young heart.
Be one with the beauty of heaven.
Dissolve into earth qi, dissolve into nature.

Your feet rest on ten thousand li of earth.
Ten thousand zhang of sky rests on your head.
Clouds and birds dance together.
The tea trees in the mountain blossom.
Ten thousand good things come from heaven.
Rest in the heart. The heart is very happy. Everything is joyful.

This qigong moves with qi. Breathing should be natural. Go into a space of emptiness. Enter into nothing. In your heart and in your mind everything is perfect. No good. No bad. No happy. No worry. Go back to your natural state. Then you can begin this qigong.

Preparation:

Assume the standing position (Fig. 1) following the Basic Preparation Instructions on page 5. Do the **ZHONGTIAN MOVEMENT** (see p. 3).

fig. 2

fig. 3

fig. 4

fig. 5

fig. 6

fig. 7

First Movement: The Spring Sun has Returned

Note: While following the instructions for the movement, imagine that the hands are to move along the rim of a vertical circle centered between the feet.

1. Gradually turn head to the left (**Fig. 2**). Following movement of head, slowly turn torso slightly to the left bending the knees. Simultaneously, allow arms and hands to float up to the left (**Fig. 3**).

2. Gradually turn torso and head to the right, leading with right shoulder. Let the movement of the torso and shoulder naturally pull right hand up and in toward the *shanzhong* (center of the chest) as right elbow drops. At the same time, following movement of torso, let left arm naturally follow, moving to the right. (Left arm remains almost straight and hand, out in front of the *dantian*.) (**Fig. 4**).

3. Then, gradually turn torso and head to the left, leading with left shoulder. Let the movement of the torso and shoulder naturally pull left hand up and in toward the *shanzhong* (center of the chest) as left elbow drops. As left hand moves up, simultaneously let right hand move down along the center to front of the *dantian*. Then, as left hand reaches the *shanzhong*, simultaneously let right hand move away from the *dantian* (**Fig. 5**).

4. Then gradually turn torso and head to the right, leading with right shoulder. Let the movement of the torso and shoulder naturally pull right hand up and in toward the *shanzhong* (center of the chest) as right elbow drops. As right hand moves up, simultaneously let left hand move down along the center to front of the *dantian*. Then as right hand reaches the *shanzhong*, simultaneously let left hand move away from the *dantian* as in **Fig. 4**.

Note: Check that the hands move along the rim of a vertical circle which is centered between the feet.

5. Repeat Steps 3 & 4, turning torso alternately from side to side as hands move along the vertical circle. Repeat as many times as desired.

6. To end this movement, as one arm is on its way up, slightly bend torso forward and allow the other arm to catch up (**Fig. 6**). Then straighten knees as hands slowly move down to sides of body (**Fig. 7**).

Points to Remember:

a) Do not think of moving arms and hands. Lead with torso. Shoulders, arms, and hands just follow. Wrists are always relaxed with hands hanging freely. Movements should be light and smooth.

b) Throughout this movement, knees are slightly bent. Weight remains centered between both feet.

c) To coordinate breathing with movement, exhale on one side and inhale on the other.

Contemplation

Try to breathe evenly. Maintain a happy demeanor. Hands move in the direction of the chest while pouring qi into the **shanzhong** *(heart point). Move gracefully, like smoke, like mist.*

The purpose of the first movement is to regulate the breathing and balance the yin/yang. Breathing is natural; the circulation of qi is smooth and unobstructed.

This first movement can stand on its own. When one is comfortable and sufficiently relaxed with the movement, it is best to simply focus on feeling one is expanding and merging with the universe. You are the universe and the universe is in you. As the planets move, the body moves. As effortlessly as the moon revolves around the earth, the body flows with the rhythm of the qi and becomes one with the universal qi.

fig. 8

fig. 9

fig. 10

Second Movement: Restoring the Sun to Its Origin

1. Bend knees slightly while bringing hips to the right and allowing arms to move to the left, with head turning right. Relax arms with relaxed wrists and hands hanging freely (**Fig. 8**).

With torso bent from the waist, hips rotate to the back towards the left as outstretched arms sweep from left to right (in the opposite direction) while head slowly turns to face left.

2. Continue with the circular movement of the hips; upon reaching the left side, gradually push the hips forward and naturally lean back. Begin to pull up as arms continue to circle to the extreme right (**Fig. 9**).

3. Allow arms to drop down to the center in front of body as arms make their way to the left to start another rotation.

4. Repeat Steps 1, 2, & 3 for as long as desired.

5. To end, gradually decrease size of movements until body is once again upright with arms and hands hanging naturally at the sides (**Fig. 10**).

Points to Remember:

a. Movements start small, gradually increase, then gradually decrease until they come to a stop.

b. To coordinate breathing with movement, inhale as arms move to the left and exhale as arms sweep to the right.

Contemplation

Focus on the waist and then move your attention to the dantian. *Relax the shoulders and the elbows, keeping knees slightly bent.*

The movement of the body is like the rising and the setting of the sun which follows the motion of the universe (like the earth revolving around the sun).

Qi will naturally develop. Do not think of anything. Relax.

For those who cannot do the full extent of the movement, it is enough to trace smaller circles with the hips remembering that the source of the movement is the dantian. *What is important is that as one lifts the body, the chest is completely open.*

fig. 11

fig. 12

fig. 13

fig. 14

Third Movement: Rediscovering the Moon

Second Movement flows into Third Movement.

1. Shift weight to the right leg and lift left heel, while rolling shoulders forward and turning head slightly to the right (**Fig. 11**). Continue rolling shoulders down while keeping arms limp and relaxed (**Fig. 12**).

2. Without stopping, shift weight to the left and lift right heel. Simultaneously, roll shoulders back and up with arms limp and relaxed with elbows slightly bent. Head turns slightly to the left (**Fig. 13**).

3. Do Steps 1 & 2 repeatedly in a continuous flowing motion while shifting weight from side to side.

4. Conclude the movement by bringing arms down to the sides and letting the body come to rest at the center (**Fig. 14**).

Points to Remember:

a) To coordinate the breathing with the movement, inhale as the shoulders move up and exhale as the shoulders move down.

b) Shoulders lead the movement with limp, relaxed arms and hands following.

c) Movements are smooth and continuous.

Contemplation

The qi has already permeated the entire body. The movements become more graceful and light; your body has become one with the qi of the universe. As the useless and unhealthy qi is gradually expelled, the qi of the universe becomes stronger. As the qi of the universe becomes stronger, it naturally expels one's useless qi. The arms and legs move slowly and gently to allow the essence of the universe to gradually merge in waves with the body.

The essence of qigong is the continuous interchange of qi between the human and the universe. This movement illustrates this principle very clearly. There is a constant exchange of qi between the universe and the practitioner. As the unused qi is expelled into the universe, the universe converts it into beneficial qi. Then the qi flows back into the body of the practitioner. The ensuing exchange that takes place ultimately has no beginning and no end.

fig. 15　　　fig. 16　　　fig. 17　　　fig. 18

Fourth Movement: Returning the Moon

1. Spread feet wider apart and bend knees slightly.

2. Hands, one following the other, trace a vertical circular path along the center of torso as follows: Right hand moves up to chest level as left hand hangs limp in front of the *dantian*. Right hand begins to trace the circle away from torso and down with the right hand flexed. At the same time, left hand moves up along the center of torso with the wrist limp. Alternately, as the left hand begins to trace the circle away from the torso and down with the left hand flexed, right hand moves up along the center of torso with the wrist limp. When the one hand is at chest level, the other is in front of the *dantian*. One circle alternately follows the other.

3. Coordinate the movement of the arms and hands with the rest of the body as follows: When bringing the relaxed right hand to chest level, twist torso to the left naturally turning head in the same direction as left hand hangs in front of the *dantian*. When bringing the relaxed left hand to chest level, twist torso to the right naturally turning head in the same direction as right hand hangs in front of the *dantian* (**Fig. 15, 16**).

4. Trace circles repeatedly for some time.

5. To end this movement, gradually slow down the movements and reduce the size of the vertical circle until both hands come to a stop in front of chest. Knees are bent; arms and wrists are relaxed with hands hanging freely (**Fig. 17**).

6. Slowly lower arms to sides while straightening knees and moving into a smaller stance (**Fig. 18**).

Points to Remember:

Relax the lower back and abdomen while doing the movement.

Contemplation

Gather all the qi from the universe into the dantian. *Try to relax the body. While doing this, it is easy for the mind to wander, so you should remain still. Think only of your* dantian. *One's emotions are like the up and down of this movement.*

The purpose of the practice of this qigong is to attain an even, calm disposition, mastering the mind, the inner self, and one's inner power. If we can maintain this even state of mind, we can attain equipoise and achieve good health.

fig. 19

fig. 20

fig. 21

fig. 22

fig. 23

FIFTH MOVEMENT:
THE SOURCE OF THOUGHT

1. Slowly shift weight to the right and turn head to face right. At the same time, move arms away from the torso as through preparing to take flight (**Fig. 19**).

2. Then bend knees and push right hip to the side; shift weight almost completely to the right leg and raise left heel. Left knee is turned out. At the same time, arms float up to about shoulder level with elbows slightly bent and wrists relaxed with hands hanging freely. Head has turned completely to the right (**Fig. 20**).

3. Release the position: gradually straighten both legs; begin to shift weight to the left as arms come down slowly and head turns to face left (**Fig. 21**).

4. Bend knees and push left hip to the side; shift weight almost completely to the left leg and raise right heel. Right knee is turned out. At the same time, arms float up to about shoulder level with elbows slightly bent and wrists relaxed with hands hanging freely. Head has turned completely to the left (**Fig. 22**).

5. Release the position: gradually straighten both legs; begin to shift weight to the right as arms come down slowly and head turns to face right.

6. Do Steps 2-5 repeatedly. Shift from one side to the other as many times as desired.

7. To conclude, bring body to upright position and let arms move down to rest at sides (**Fig. 23**).

Points to Remember:

a. When raising arms, let them move naturally and float up to a comfortable height.

b. Do not force the sideward movements of waist and hips. Remain relaxed and let them move naturally.

c. To coordinate breathing with the movement, exhale when bending knees and pushing hip to the side, and inhale when straightening knees.

CONTEMPLATION

Your mind is like a carefree bird, flying, merging with the universe. The unhealthy qi is almost totally gone from your body. Pure qi is circulating in your body and making you one with nature. Your body can now receive sustenance and nutrition from nature. As you condense the pure qi of nature into your body, all worries and negativities dissolve.

The main purpose of this qigong is to help your body. This movement has no deeper meaning. It is easy to do and easy to understand. One simply returns to nature. The word "Spring" (in this qigong, "Return to Spring") refers to nature — a return to nature, the original state. It also signifies beauty, goodness, vitality.

The key to maintaining good health is to maintain a lightness of being. Do not think too much. It is best to always try to maintain an even disposition.

fig. 24 front

fig. 24 side

fig. 25 front

fig. 25 side

Sixth Movement: Sunrise Brings Back the Light

1. (**Fig. 24 front & side**) Gradually bend knees and let the body slowly collapse forward at an angle of about 30° to 45° from the vertical.

Chest and abdomen are relaxed and collapsed; lower back is rounded.

Relaxed hands and arms bent at the elbows hang naturally down; slightly move forward as body bends forward.

Let head hang naturally.

2. (**Fig. 25 front & side**) Push up with the legs, straightening legs and body.

Head tilts back slightly and chest and abdomen are open.

Arms move back and hang naturally at sides.

3. Repeat Steps 1 and 2 as many times as they feel right or comfortable. To conclude, stop with body in vertical position with arms and hands resting naturally at sides.

Points to Remember:

a) What is important is the movement of the torso. Like a balloon, the body deflates when coming down and expands when moving up. Do not think of moving the arms; just let them move naturally following the movement of the torso.

b) Breathe naturally. While exhaling, visualise bringing energy to the *dantian* as the body collapses forward. While inhaling, visualise bringing up the energy from the *dantian* to the *shanzhong* as the body comes upright and the chest and abdomen open up.

Contemplation

Beam the body's qi to the qi of the dantian. *As they reflect each other, this will result in even greater energy. Once you have attained a high level of skill, you can practice slowly moving the qi from the* dantian *to the* shanzhong *and then move it slowly back to the* dantian. *Repeat; slowly move the qi as you raise and lower it.*

Relax your shoulders; pull up slightly from the top of your head; lower the hips. It is as though you were between heaven and earth. The gentle qi permeates and intermingles – like rain, like snow, like wind, like mist.

All phenomena in the universe arise from stillness and motion. Motion and stillness come from the movement of the universe: truth and non-truth, non-truth and truth. Motion is like stillness and stillness is like motion. Within the motion is a point of stillness. At the heart of the stillness is a non-ending motion.

The heart moves but the mind is still. The mind moves but the heart is still. When you ponder over a problem, your mind maintains equanimity and peace. In this way, you will not go to extremes or lose hope in yourself when analyzing a problem. You achieve balance in thinking with your heart. Inevitably, one knows what is helpful and what is harmful.

When one makes decisions with others in mind, he is acting from his own greatness as a human being. His heart is full of love — he understands nature, the universe, its deeper meanings, origin, and future.

fig. 26

fig. 27

fig. 28

fig. 29

fig. 30

fig. 31

Seventh Movement: Flying and Gazing at the Nine Levels of Heaven

1. Shift weight to right leg while keeping both legs straight. Left heel is raised and toes lightly touch the ground. Simultaneously, slightly expand arms out to the sides with wrists relaxed and hands hanging freely (**Fig. 26**).

2. Turn to face left and allow body to move up and down, bending and straightening both knees in a bouncing fashion while keeping weight on right leg, left heel raised throughout. Coordinate the bouncing movement with arms and hands in the following manner: Gently lift wrists allowing hands to hang limp when knees bend (**Fig. 27**). Then lightly push down with heels of flexed hands when knees straighten (**Fig. 28**). Naturally bend at the elbows when raising wrists; arms and hands remain relaxed. Head is still turned to left. Bounce as many times as desired.

3. After a few bounces, shift weight to left leg while keeping both legs straight. Right heel is raised and toes lightly touch the ground. At the same time, slightly expand arms out to the sides. Repeat the bouncing movement with weight on the left leg (**Fig. 29, 30, 31**).

4. To end, straighten both legs while still keeping weight on left foot; arms are almost straight with hands flexed and pressing down; head remains turned to the right. Hold this position for some time.

Points To Remember:

Do the bouncing movement lightly and in a pulsating rhythm. There should be a feeling of lightness. Smile throughout the movement.

Contemplation

Not every man can reach nine levels of heaven. When one's qi is in a pure state, one embodies the truth. One can travel the "six directions" (everywhere) and rise up to the nine (highest) levels of heaven. Truth is embodied in man. Man holds the source of highest understanding. If a human being is able to grasp the highest and the deepest truths, he can bring himself to the highest level of Heaven. Imagine what kind of a world it is there. Let your mind fly to the world beyond your body and find your bliss.

The meaning of life is found not only in happiness but also in sorrow. Life is sadness and happiness, separation and reunion, up and down, ebb and flow. The worries of our life, the emotions of our life are like the up-and-down movements of our hands. They may be heavy, they may be light. They are full. They are empty.

When you lose everything and seem to have sunk to the lowest point of your life, having practiced this qigong, you will not forget your happy moments, you will not forget those who have helped you. When your morale is high, you will remember those who need your help. This is equipoise. This is yin and yang. This is the universe. This is the world. This forms your colorful and extraordinary life.

The ninth level of Heaven signifies man's highest attainment. The attainment of this level in this lifetime or in the succeeding lifetime depends on one's thoughts, actions, and intentions on this earth in this lifetime. What is important is that in this lifetime, one can appreciate the many colors that one sees in one's life. It is the appreciation of the design of one's life that brings one slowly to the highest level of attainment.

fig. 32

fig. 33

fig. 34

fig. 35

fig. 36

Eighth Movement: Cultivating Your Dan and Higher Self

1. From the ending of the Seventh Movement, turn torso to face right by pivoting on the ball of the right foot and shifting weight to right leg. Begin to turn left foot in the same direction while raising heel off the floor; turn foot over so left leg rests on top of overturned foot. At the same time, bend elbows out to the side to bring hands in front of chest (**Fig. 32**).

2. With foot in position and hands in front of chest as your starting point (**Fig. 32**), bend the right leg simultaneously pushing down gently with heels of hands (**Fig. 33**).

3. Then, slightly raise the body and release hand position; hands are limp.

4. Keeping weight on right leg, continue to alternate Steps 2 and 3 in a bouncing fashion as many times as desired. Sole of left foot remains turned up with the top side of the toes touching the floor to provide balance.

5. To do the transition movement to the left, turn 180° and shift weight from right to left leg as follows: after the downward movement of the last repetition on the right side, pivot on the ball of the left foot followed by the right till body completely faces the opposite side; the weight now rests on the left leg so that the right foot is free to turn upside down with the top and tip of foot touching the ground. While turning, gradually bring limp wrists to chest level and proceed to do the bouncing movement as done on the opposite side (**Fig. 34 & 35**).

6. Conclude this movement by turning to face forward with both knees bent, and weight centered in both legs. Simultaneously, while keeping knees bent, allow arms and elbows to rise to chest level, with back of fingertips touching. Then bring hands to prayer position while straightening both legs, (**Fig. 36**).

Points to Remember:

Keep the range of the hand movements small; keep elbows always bent.

Contemplation

As the qi begins to flow effortlessly though the body and collects in the **dantian**, **dan** *is cultivated. The Higher Self inevitably begins to shine forth.*

This is the mystery of the human being — that the more one is anchored to life enriched by qi, the more naturally one's divinity surfaces; the more clearly one stands between heaven and earth.

In doing this movement, it is important for the toes to be in proper position. As the hands push down, the qi flows through the body and out the **yongquan** *(center of soles of the feet) to start a new circle from the* **baihui** *down. If one is unable to keep this position, it is permissible to find a more comfortable position for the toes.*

fig. 37

fig. 38

fig. 39

fig. 40

fig. 41

Ninth Movement: The Moon Rises and Shines on the West Chamber

1. From prayer position, slowly turn fingers forward and extend arms away from the body. Keeping tips of fingers together, part hands forming a circle with the arms (**Fig. 37**).

2. Raise arms above the head (**Fig. 38**).

3. Keeping hands above head and body upright, exhale relaxing chest and abdomen while bending knees and bringing palms together (**Fig. 39**).

4. While inhaling, straighten legs, bringing body back upright, parting palms, with fingertips lightly touching (**Fig. 40**).

Continue to alternate Steps 3 and 4, moving body up and down as palms open and close. Repeat as many times as desired. End with legs straight and bring palms together while slowly lowering them back to prayer position (**Fig. 41**).

Points to Remember:

This movement is better done slowly. As the body moves up, imagine qi expanding throughout the whole body up to the tips of toes and fingers.
As the body moves down, imagine qi contracting back to the *dantian*.

Contemplation

The qi circulates and reaches to the end of your extremities. You live peacefully and enjoy the happiness of your life. You grasp the meaning of nature and understand your relationship with it.

When doing this movement, relax the abdomen as the body contracts, thus allowing the qi to flow into the **dantian**.

fig. 42 fig. 43 fig. 44 fig. 45

fig. 46 fig. 47 fig. 48 fig. 49

Tenth Movement: The True Moonlight

1. Keeping body upright and facing forward with hands together, as in **Fig. 41**, slowly turn head from side to side starting with the left.

2. After turning head two or three times, begin to push hands in the direction opposite to that in which head is turning: as head turns left, hands push to the right (**Fig. 42**) and as head turns right, hands push to the left (**Fig. 43**). Move hands only as far as they can easily go without exerting force.

Note: This is a movement of the head and hands. Keep torso facing directly forward throughout this movement – do not twist shoulders and/or waist from side to side.

3. After two or three repetitions of the head and hands movement, gradually increase hand movements until hands are moving as far as they can go on each side.

4. As hand movements increase in range, widen the stance to facilitate the movements as they become larger: push hands to one side, and move head and weight in the opposite direction. Repeat the movements from side to side as many times as desired (**Fig. 44 & 45**).

5. Gradually decrease the size of the range of movements until body is standing straight with weight evenly distributed (**Fig. 46**).

6. As hands come to a stop in front of the center of the chest, keep palms and fingers together. Then lower hands and turn them outward until fingers point down; then, start separating palms until they face up in front of the *dantian*. (**Fig. 47**).

7. Lean at first slightly forward to spread arms sideward, then even more forward with wrists limp (**Fig. 48**). Without pausing, begin to pull back allowing the hands to glide down, gradually closing fingers to form a hollow fist (with thumb and forefinger touching) till the body comes to rest in an upright position (**Fig. 49**).

Points to Remember:

a) At the start of the movement breathe naturally. As the range of the movements gradually build up, breathing deepens and increases in intensity and in rhythm with the movement. As the movements decrease in size and intensity, the breathing decreases.

b) As each sideward movement of the head is completed, gently stretch the neck by very slightly pushing the chin forward.

c) When the sideward movements are at their largest, mark the midpoint with an inhalation or an exhalation.

d) The movements are smooth and even throughout.

f) As the qi becomes very full and very strong, the breathing can be very slow. Two to three of the sideward movements can be completed in the space of a single exhalation.

When doing the maximum movements very slowly, a humming sound can be made through the nose. The sound vibration helps the body to relax even more.

Contemplation

The true moonlight is the light that shines everywhere — that which can be seen through the eyes of the heart. It is also the light that shines in your heart.

fig. 50   fig. 51   fig. 52

Eleventh Movement: The Reblooming of Spring Flower

1. Turn head slightly from side to side, starting slowly and then intensifying, gradually increasing the speed and range of movement. At the same time, from the hollow fist at the close of the preceding movement, release hands, keeping them relaxed and limp to move naturally in harmony with the head movements.

2. As the movements intensify, drop the body weight and bend the knees, while swinging from side to side, keeping the hips and waist relaxed. The arms and the head naturally follow the momentum and move in the opposite direction to the body weight (**Fig. 50 & 51**).

3. Repeat the side to side movements as many times as desired.

4. To end, gradually make movements slower and smaller until body comes to a stop. Stand naturally with arms hanging at sides (**Fig. 52**).

Points to Remember:

a) Smile throughout the movement feeling playful and carefree.

b) This movement is important for exercising the waist and hips as well as making the spine flexible.

Contemplation

Allow the pure qi in your body to circulate; turn it, bend it, rock it. The movement should neither be too large nor hastily done. This movement does not require concentration. Let go of all inhibitions; let the body enjoy the rocking movement.

fig. 53

fig. 54

fig. 55

fig. 56

fig. 57

fig. 58

TWELFTH MOVEMENT:
BILLOWING SILK LIKE AN
ENDLESS ROAD

1. From the last position of the previous movement, keep shoulders and hands relaxed and raise arms slightly out to the sides to about head level, (**Fig. 53**). Without stopping, turn palms up and open the chest: open arms wider, while tilting back head. Hold this position for a few seconds (**Fig. 54**).

2. Lean forward from the hips; turn over hands so that palms face down. Wrists are relaxed and hands hang freely. Keep head aligned with torso while looking down. Knees are locked (**Fig. 55**).

3. Slowly bring the hands down to the sides and bring body to upright position (**Fig. 56**).

4. While inhaling, expand the chest; feel the body expand; leading with the elbows, allow arms to float away from the body as it expands (**Fig. 57**).

5. While exhaling, the body contracts relaxing the chest, the lower back, and bending the knees slightly. Bring arms closer to the body and let them hang loosely while the head gently drops (**Fig. 58**).

6. Repeat steps Steps 4 & 5 as many times as desired. End this movement with body upright and arms hanging at sides (**Fig. 56**).

Points To Remember:
Move slowly and breathe naturally.

CONTEMPLATION

This movement does not require much thought. Everything follows what is natural. Relax.

The title "Billowing Silk Like an Endless Road" is the description of the qi moving in the body of one who has returned to Nature. The qi moves as smoothly as the finest silk forever billowing in the wind like an endless road.

fig. 59

Thirteenth Movement: The Universe Trembles

Whole body is relaxed. Arms hang loosely at sides. Vibrate the body by bouncing up and down to release excess qi andthus balance the qi in the body. If desired, intensify the movement by lifting and striking heels on the ground in quick succession (**Fig. 59**).

Points To Remember:
This movement is for harmonising energy and for returning your body to a state of comfort in a natural way. The entire body -- knees, back, arms, and neck -- is relaxed and loose throughout the movement.

Contemplation

Empty your mind. Let yourself go and be natural.

As you naturally bounce up and down, allow the qi to circulate and spread throughout the body. As the qi moves more vigorously, it is further empowered to purify the body as it improves the circulation of the blood. The movement of the qi itself is what keeps the qi fresh.

Not resisting movement and change in one's life enables one to stay fresh and open, as well as to be always ready to welcome the infinite possibilities and variety the universe offers. When the heart is open enough to appreciate the limitless colors that life offers, life becomes effortless and becomes a joyful ride.

fig. 60

Fourteenth Movement: Qi Returns to Spring

No physical movement is required. Just stand still and concentrate on the *dantian*. Imagine energy from the *dantian* expanding throughout the whole body. This is when Qi Returns to Spring – how one goes back to the beginning (**Fig. 60**).

Contemplation

Let the qi return to the dantian. *As one's mood becomes stable and happy, concentrate on the* dantian. *From there, watch the qi expand to all the parts of the body – to the* yongquan *(soles of the feet) and up to the* ming-tang *(the third eye). The qi permeates the body and spreads out to the* laogong *(the palms of the hands).*

From there, let the qi continue to expand to the ends of the universe. Revel in the immensity of the universe. It is the qi that powers the universe. Slowly, the qi travels back in a spiral, like a spinning milky way, towards and into the dantian. *Take several deep breaths.*

fig. 61

THE CLOSING MOVEMENT:

Qi has returned to the *dantian* (**Fig. 61**).

Breathe deeply a few times. Conclude with the **ZHONGTIAN MOVEMENT** (**see p. 3**).

Smiling while doing this qigong puts you in an altered state. After the closing, gently and gradually return to normal waking consciousness.

Glossary of Terms

A
acupuncture – traditional Chinese medical treatment consisting of puncturing the body with needles at points along the meridians of qi to cure disease and/or remove pain.

B
baihui – the acupuncture point located at the top of the head, the center of the crown.

bodhi – the tree under which Sakyamuni Buddha achieved enlightenment.

buddha – the title given to one who is fully realized, awakened, or enlightened; one with God.

C
cultivation – often used when referring to the care of the entire man or woman, i.e., the body, the mind, the emotions, and spirit as in the care and cultivation of a garden or farm.

consciousness – state of awareness.

Consciousness – the intelligent, pure, supreme energy that pervades all.

D
dan – seed of condensed qi located below the navel in the dantian.

dantian – the storage place of qi in the body, about two inches below the navel.

dazhui – acupuncture point at the back, the seventh cervical vertebra.

E
"eight directions" – a Chinese idiom for all directions.

enlightenment – the state of full realization of being one with all, with God.

F
five gateways – the entry points of qi through the palms of the hands (**laogong**), the soles of the feet (**yongquan**) and the crown (**baihui**).

G
gong – effort, exertion

H
hui chun – return to spring

J
jingluo – meridians or passageways of qi in the body.

jiu zhuan – nine turns.

L
lotus – flower symbolic of enlightenment and purity; refers to a sitting position often used for yoga.

laogong – the acupoint located at the center of the palms.

li – a unit of measurement equivalent to 1/3 millimeter; .05 gram; .666 square meters.

M
meditation – a method or practice to awaken consciousness.

meridians – pathways of qi; jinglou.

ming-men – acupoint located at the back directly behind the navel.

ming-tang – point just behind the yin-tang (point between the eyebrows).

"mouth of tiger" – the part of the hand between the thumb and the pointing or second finger.

N

ni-wuan – the point located in the head which is the intersection of lines drawn from the center of the forehead (**yin-tang**) and the top of the head (**baihui**).

"Ninth Level of Heaven" – the highest level of heaven.

P

pre-natal qi – is the innate qi received from our biological parents, which has both weak and strong elements.

post-natal qi – this refers to pathogenic elements that affect the health after birth.

Q

qi – vital energy or life force.

qigong – the principle of the continuous interchange of qi with qi as in that between man and the universe; the form or practice of actively engaging in this continuous interchange; the state of merging, being in the flow as in a meditative state.

R

Ren Mai – the meridian that flows along the center of the front torso.

S

saint – a spirit of a departed one in heaven; a godly person; one recognized primarily for purity and holiness.

shanzhong – acupoint located at the heart area or center of chest between the nipples.

Sheng Zhen – unconditional, pure love; most sacred, highest truth.

T

taiji – the unity of yin and yang; where yin and yang meet.

"ten thousand" – a Chinese idiom for everything.

W

wuji – before the beginning of time before the duality of yin and yang.

X

xing – character; the growth that comes from experiencing and knowing nature; enlightened consciousness.

xiuxing – contemplating, striving, and working towards enlightenment; the act of walking a path to enlightenment by applying what one has learned from self-inquiry and contemplation.

Y

yang – literally, "the sunny side of the mountain'; one of the fundamental polar forces that organize the universe. Yang manifests as form, light, activity, heavenly, masculine, and the like.

yi qi – primordial qi, first qi.

yin – literally, "the shady side of the mountain"; one of the fundamental polar forces that organize the universe. Yin manifests as substance, darkness, stillness, of the earth, feminine, and the like.

yin-tang – acupoint located at the center of the eyebrows.

yongquan – acupoint located at the center of the soles of the feet.

yuan – primordial, original.

Z

zhang – unit of measurement equivalent to one palm (of the hand).

zhongchong – acupoint located at the tip of the third or middle finger.

zhongtian – to flow through freely – to be able to pass free of obstacles within oneself and others, to arrive at Oneness.

ABOUT THE MASTER

Li Jun Feng embodies the spirit of Sheng Zhen. The moving force behind bringing the Sheng Zhen practices to the world, he is the head and principal teacher of the International Sheng Zhen Society.

Li Jun Feng is perhaps best known as having been the head coach for the world-renowned Beijing Wushu (Martial Arts) Team and the National Wushu Team of the People's Republic of China for over 15 years. Under his leadership, these teams won numerous laurels and unprecedented honor to the country. During those years he also achieved international fame as a martial arts film actor and director.

Master Li is Dean of Qigong at the Academy of Oriental Medicine at Austin, Texas, U.S.A. Currently residing in Austin, he travels extensively to bring the practice of Sheng Zhen Wuji Yuan Gong to people around the world. In more than 20 countries, he has taught and shared what he has learned and how he has been transformed by this remarkable practice.

Today, Master Li works as council member of the World Academic Society of Medical Qigong and before, he used to serve as advisor to the Qigong Science Research Association of China.

ABOUT THE ISZS

The International Sheng Zhen Society is a non-profit foundation formed to promote the spirit of Sheng Zhen — the spirit of unconditional love. It propagates the Sheng Zhen practices throughout the world. Its work is supported through the offerings of all those who believe in and want to help in this loving work. Out of a spirit of sharing and gratitude, people offer their time, their bodies, their skills, and their material resources to expand the spirit of Sheng Zhen.

For more information on courses and retreats offered around the world as well as instructional books, audio and video materials on the Sheng Zhen practices and philosophy, visit our website at www.shengzhen.org.

More Information

www.shengzhen.org